A Guide to the Wallace Collection

Introduction

The Wallace Collection is a national museum which displays the art collections brought together by the first four Marquesses of Hertford and the son of the 4th Marquess, Sir Richard Wallace. It was bequeathed to the British nation by Lady Wallace, Sir Richard's widow, in 1897.

Among the Collection's treasures are an outstanding array of 18th-century French pictures, porcelain and furniture, many important 17th and 19th-century paintings, medieval and Renaissance works of art and the finest collection of princely arms and armour in Britain. The Wallace Collection is displayed in Hertford House, formerly the main London residence of the Marquesses of Hertford and Sir Richard Wallace. It was opened to the public as a museum in 1900.

Hertford House

The Hertford family's association with Hertford House began in 1797 when the 2nd Marquess of Hertford bought the leasehold of the building. The 2nd Marchioness was a great hostess, and in the first decades of the 19th century Hertford House was much visited by fashionable London society. The 3rd Marquess preferred to live at his other London residences, Dorchester House and St Dunstan's, and the 4th Marquess, who lived most of his life in Paris, used the building largely as a store for his ever expanding art collection. The 4th Marquess died in 1870 and his illegitimate son, Richard Wallace, bought Hertford House from his cousin, the 5th Marquess, in the following year.

Wallace, who had been brought up in Paris by his father and grandmother, moved into Hertford House in 1875 after extensive alterations to the building had been carried out. Under Wallace and his wife Hertford House again became a fashionable place to visit, though not because the Wallaces were renowned hosts but because of their fabulous art collection. Wallace died in Paris in 1890, but his widow continued to live at Hertford House, aided by her secretary John Murray Scott, until her own death in 1897. Between 1897 and 1900 the former private residence was converted into a public museum. Galleries replaced the stabling, coach-houses and smoking room as well as some private rooms on the first floor. Many less radical changes have been made since the museum opened.

The 4th Marquess (left), Madame Oger and Richard Wallace at Bagatelle, c.1855

The Founders of the Wallace Collection

Although some important works of art now in the Wallace Collection were acquired in the 18th century by the 1st and 2nd Marquesses of Hertford (for example some paintings by Canaletto, Reynolds and Gainsborough), the first member of the family to show a real interest in art was the 3rd Marquess. A friend of the Prince Regent, later King George IV, he acquired important 17th-century Dutch paintings, French furniture, gilt bronzes and Sèvres porcelain.

It was, however, his son the 4th Marquess, one of the greatest collectors of the 19th century, who determined the essential character of the Wallace Collection we

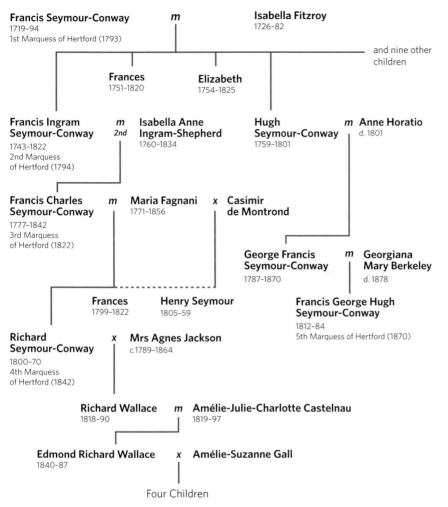

Francis Seymour-Conway
1719–94
1st Marquess of Hertford (1793)

m

Isabella Fitzroy
1726–82

and nine other children

Frances
1751–1820

Elizabeth
1754–1825

Francis Ingram Seymour-Conway
1743–1822
2nd Marquess of Hertford (1794)

m
2nd

Isabella Anne Ingram-Shepherd
1760–1834

Hugh Seymour-Conway
1759–1801

m

Anne Horatio
d. 1801

Francis Charles Seymour-Conway
1777–1842
3rd Marquess of Hertford (1822)

m

Maria Fagnani
1771–1856

x

Casimir de Montrond

George Francis Seymour-Conway
1787–1870

m

Georgiana Mary Berkeley
d. 1878

Frances
1799–1822

Henry Seymour
1805–59

Francis George Hugh Seymour-Conway
1812–84
5th Marquess of Hertford (1870)

Richard Seymour-Conway
1800–70
4th Marquess of Hertford (1842)

x

Mrs Agnes Jackson
c.1789–1864

Richard Wallace
1818–90

m

Amélie-Julie-Charlotte Castelnau
1819–97

Edmond Richard Wallace
1840–87

x

Amélie-Suzanne Gall

Four Children

William Robert Symonds, *Sir Richard Wallace,* **1885** (67.6 x 56.2cm) [P578]

Charles Auguste Lebourg, *Lady Wallace,* **1872** (h. 71cm) [S45]

see today. Brought up in Paris by his mother after she separated from his father, the 4th Marquess later lived in style in a large apartment on the Rue Laffitte and at Bagatelle, a chateau in the Bois de Boulogne. His art collecting combined aspects of both French and English taste and his enormous wealth (gained largely from estates in England and Ireland) enabled him to indulge that taste to the full. His acquisitions included the great majority of the paintings, porcelain and furniture now in the Wallace Collection as well as the Oriental arms and armour. He bought art on such a large scale that much of his collection was kept in storage rather than on display, though he was an important lender to contemporary exhibitions.

The 4th Marquess never married, but he did have illegitimate children. His son Richard Wallace, after spending his earliest years in London, became in Paris his father's assistant and adviser, particularly in matters relating to art. In 1870 he inherited his father's collection as well as properties in France, England and Ireland. A great philanthropist, Wallace was knighted in 1871 for his charitable services during the Siege of Paris. In 1872 he brought over to London many of the works of art inherited from his father, to which he had added important collections of medieval and Renaissance objects including European arms and armour. While Hertford House was being converted to accommodate his collection (1872–5), much of Wallace's collection was exhibited at the Bethnal Green Museum where it was a popular sensation. In 1890 he bequeathed all his property to his widow Lady Wallace who on her own death seven years later left the collection at Hertford House to the nation, almost certainly fulfilling her husband's wishes. She left most of the rest of her property, which included many fine works of art, to her secretary John Murray Scott.

The Entrance Hall

The Entrance Hall contains marble busts of the three principal Founders of the Wallace Collection, Richard Seymour-Conway, 4th Marquess of Hertford (1800–70), his son Sir Richard Wallace (1818–90) and, in the lobby, Lady Wallace, who bequeathed the contents of Hertford House to the British Nation on her death in 1897. It was refurbished in 1994 to its appearance in this photograph of c.1890, the room still looks almost exactly as it did in Sir Richard Wallace's day. In 1878 Queen Victoria's favourite Prime Minister, Benjamin Disraeli, Earl of Beaconsfield, visited Hertford House and signed Sir Richard Wallace's Visitors' Book 'Beaconsfield in this palace of genius, fancy and taste'.

c.1890

Edwin Landseer, *The Arab Tent*, 1866
(153.6 x 226.4cm) [P376]

The Arab Tent depicts a menagerie of contented animals. An Arab mare and foal lie on an oriental carpet. A monkey and a baboon, which clutches an orange and wears an earring, nestle among palm leaves on the roof of a tent. Persian hounds sleep on a soft bed of rugs and skins. Landseer, who specialised in animal subjects, sold *The Arab Tent* to the Prince of Wales (later Edward VII). He was also extremely popular with ordinary Victorians who knew his paintings through exhibitions and engravings.

Louis François Roubiliac, *Charles I, King of England*, 1759 (71cm high) [S23]

Roubiliac was perhaps the finest sculptor of portrait busts of 18th-century England. This is a posthumous portrait of King Charles I (1625–49) sculpted for George Selwyn of Matson whose adopted daughter and legatee was the 3rd Marchioness of Hertford. The bust was recorded in the 18th century as standing on a pedestal commemorating Charles I's visit to Matson in 1643.

The Front State Room

The London Town House

When Hertford House was the home of Sir Richard and Lady Wallace important visitors would be received in the Front State Room. This room was refurbished in 1994 to return it as closely as possible to its appearance in the Wallaces' time.

*c.*1890

Although some of the furniture shown in the photograph is no longer in the Collection, the magnificent chandelier made by Jean-Jacques Caffiéri and the portrait of the Prince of Wales by Hoppner, a gift to the 3rd Marquess of Hertford, are once again prominent features of the room.

Joshua Reynolds, *Lady Elizabeth Seymour-Conway*, 1781 (60.7 x 46.5cm) [P31]

The 1st Marquess commissioned Reynolds to paint his daughters, Elizabeth and Frances. Elizabeth never married; Frances married Henry, Earl of Lincoln, in 1775.

Joshua Reynolds, *Frances, Countess of Lincoln*, 1781/2 (60.7 x 46.5cm) [P33]

Thomas Lawrence, *Margaret, Countess of Blessington*, 1822 (91.5 x 67cm) [P558]

Margaret, Countess of Blessington is a portrait of Margaret Power, an Irish beauty who married her second husband, the Earl of Blessington, in 1818 when she was 21. Four years later she took a lover, Alfred, comte d'Orsay, who became her constant companion. Lady Blessington was one of the most celebrated society women of her time. She held a famous literary salon and was an acquaintance of Byron, who wrote that her portrait had 'set all London raving.'

Thomas Sully, *Queen Victoria,* **1838**
(142.5 x 112.5cm) [P564]

This portrait of Queen Victoria was painted the year after she ascended the throne. Sully, an American citizen, was commissioned by an anglophile society in Philadelphia to paint a portrait of the Queen, of which this is a reduced version. It was commissioned by a London firm of print publishers who intended to publish engravings after the painting. Sully kept a journal in which he noted his impressions of the Queen: 'She is short, 5 feet 1 & ¼ of an inch – of good form, particularly the neck and bosom – plump, but not fat. Neatly formed head... A lovely artless mouth when at rest... And to sum up all... I should say decidedly, that she is quite pretty.'

John Hoppner, *George IV as Prince of Wales,* **1792**
(126.5 x 100.4cm) [P563]

George IV as Prince of Wales portrays the Prince aged 30. He showed great favour to Lord Yarmouth (later 3rd Marquess) and, in 1811, gave him this portrait. It may have been exhibited at the Royal Academy in 1792. It shows George in 'plain clothes', rather than formal robes, and emphasises the easy elegance for which the Prince was famous. The picture has retained its 1810 frame by the London carver and gilder John Smith, bearing the Prince of Wales's feathers and motto *ich dien* ('I serve').

The Back State Room

c.1890

The Rococo of Louis XV and Madame de Pompadour

This room is a tribute to the patronage of King Louis XV (1715–74) and his mistress, Madame de Pompadour. It displays some of the greatest examples in the Wallace Collection of rococo art, which flourished under their patronage. 'Rococo' derives from 'rocaille', which means loose stones or rocky ground. This exuberant, animated style brings the garden indoors, with fountain imagery, rampant sprays of foliage and flowers, swirling scrolls and asymmetry.

Sir Richard Wallace used the Back State Room to entertain guests to Hertford House. During his lifetime the walls were decorated with painted panelling and mirrors; the great chandelier, by Jacques Caffiéri, dating from 1751, has hung in the room ever since.

Jacques Caffiéri, Chandelier, 1751 (w. 190cm) [F83]

The twelve-light chandelier is made of gilt bronze.
It was given by Louis XV to his eldest daughter,
Louise-Elisabeth. The strong twisting forms are like
plants which have grown wild. Beneath each arm is
a posy of flowers with a rose; the candleholders are
shaped like vases.

**Garniture of vases, Sèvres porcelain,
1758-9** (central vase h. 48.9cm) [C251-3]

In 1759 Louis XV became sole proprietor of
Sèvres and appears to have visited the factory
in December and acquired these three vases.
The entwined green snakes with gilded scales
and zig-zag and peacock patterns are striking
and unusual, while the scenes of
soldiers show that France
was engaged in the Seven
Years' War.

The porcelain here comes from the royal
factory of Sèvres, founded at Vincennes in
1740 and moved to Sèvres in 1756. It is made
of soft-paste porcelain, with a wonderful
creamy body, but which was immensely
fragile in the kiln. Each piece was moulded
or thrown, then fired, glazed, had the ground
colour applied, then the painted decoration
and finally the gilding. In between each
process it was fired at least once (and the
gilding could be fired as many as three times
to get the depth for tooling with naturalistic
details or a variety of patterns).

Vase Candelabra, Sèvres porcelain, 1757-8
(h. 39.3cm) [C250]

This elephant vase candelabra is one of a pair which
forms a garniture with the gondola-shaped pot-pourri
vase and may have belonged to Madame de Pompadour.
The naturalistic detailing of the elephants' heads gives a
distinctive character to each animal.

At a time when washing was minimal, pot pourri was used
to perfume rooms and mask unpleasant smells. Much
French 18th-century interior decoration was inspired by
the garden. A pot-pourri vase completed the scheme by
bringing the scent of flowers indoors.

Cup and Saucer, Sèvres porcelain, 1765
(h. 8.3cm, d. 15.3cm) [C362]

Used for tea, coffee or chocolate, this piece has rare and bizarre shell-like painted decoration. It was probably painted by Méreaud le Jeune, who specialized in friezes, flower sprays, roses, ribbons and designs after fabrics. The bizarreness of its decoration brings to life the thirst for novelty that fuelled innovation in the decorative arts in 18th-century France.

Inkstand, Sèvres porcelain, 1758–9 (w. 38cm) [C488]

This ingenious Sèvres inkstand was given by Louis XV to his daughter Marie-Adélaide. The terrestrial globe contained the inkwell, the crown of France contained a bell and the cushion on which it sits contained the sponge for wiping your pen nib, and the celestial globe the gilded orb of a sand shaker for drying ink on the page. Imagine placing the sand shaker back in its globe and seeing the stars twinkling in the candlelight as the gold shone through the piercings.

Astronomical clock, French, c.1750 (h. 294.5cm) [F98]

This monumental astronomical clock was made for Jean Paris de Monmartel, banker to the court of Louis XV. Exceptionally, an engraving shows Montmartel sitting in his grand cabinet on the first floor of the Hôtel Mazarin, the clock in the background indicating his taste for opulent works of art in the latest taste. Louis XV is known to have taken delight in such complex, mechanical pieces, and famously had an astronomical clock in a case by Jacques and Philippe Caffiéri which took Passemant twelve years to design. Monmartel's clock enables you to tell the time in hours, minutes and seconds, and solar time, as well as indicating the signs of the Zodiac, the date, the day of the week, the time at any place in the northern hemisphere, the age of the moon and its current phase and the position of the sun in the sky, or the moon if it is night. The movement and astronomical train were designed by the inventor, Alexandre Fortier, and made by Michel Stollewerk.

Jean-Baptiste Oudry, *The Dead Wolf*, 1721
(193 x 260cm) [P626]

The Dead Roe and *The Dead Wolf* are the masterpieces of Oudry's early career. They would probably have hung in a room used for dining. Animals killed in the hunt, fruit gathered from the land and a tempting *pâté en croûte*

Jean-Baptiste Oudry, *The Dead Roe*, 1721
(193 x 260cm) [P630]

decorated with *fleurs de lis*, the French royal emblem, are displayed in monumental settings. Oudry's palette favours whites, pale blues, pinks, blue-greens and greys. The composition combines objects in a picturesque arrangement.

Antoine-Robert Gaudreaus and Jacques Caffiéri, Commode (chest-of-drawers), 1739 (w. 88.8cm) [F86]

Perhaps the finest and most important example of the Rococo style in the decorative arts in the Wallace Collection, this commode was delivered by Gaudreaus for Louis XV's new bedchamber of his appartément intérieur in April 1739. A design for the commode attributed to the sculptor Sébastien-Antoine Slodtz, now in the Bibliothèque Nationale, reveals that the mounts

were originally intended to be much more symmetrical. However, as executed by the master bronzier Caffiéri, they are wildly exuberant and seem to grow organically in every direction over the surface of the commode. Louis XV, as he lay dying on his bed, is said to have thought that in the flickering firelight, the mounts looked like the flames of hell. The commode was inherited by the King's First Gentleman of the Bedchamber, the duc d'Aumont, who probably replaced the original red and grey marble top with this one of serpentine marble.

The Dining Room

Eighteenth-Century Still-lifes and Portraits

The room is appropriately furnished with still-life paintings depicting fruit and game. It also contains portraits by Houdon and Nattier of four aristocratic French women of the ancient régime, two of whom were victims of the Terror of the French Revolution. The doors to the Hall, closed in 1897, have been reopened to enable the visitor to experience walking through the house to the garden.

As its name suggests, the Dining Room was the room in which Sir Richard and Lady Wallace would generally take their meals, other than breakfast, for which they had a special room (now the Cloakroom). The furniture seen in the photograph, taken around 1890, no longer forms part of the Collection.

c.1890

Jean Antoine Houdon, *Bust of Madame de Sérilly*, **1782** (h. 62cm) [S26]

Madame de Sérilly was aged 19 when her portrait bust was made. She was a maid of honour to Marie-Antoinette and a devoted friend of Louis XVI's sister, Madame Elisabeth. In 1794, during the Terror she and her husband were accused of plotting with Madame Elisabeth to assist Louis XVI (by then dead). By declaring falsely that Madame de Sérilly was pregnant Madame Elisabeth helped her friend escape the guillotine.

Houdon (1741–1828) was the foremost French sculptor of the second half of the 18th century, best known for his remarkably vivid portrait busts. After the Revolution he continued working but gradually fell out of favour.

Jean-Marc Nattier, *The comtesse de Tillières*, **1750** (80 x 63cm) [P453]

The comtesse de Tillières is an example of a new type of informal portrait in French painting which aimed, above all, at 'naturalness'. The comtesse wears a simple powdered coiffure. Her natural expression and her relaxed seated pose give the portrait an air of intimacy.

Jean-Marc Nattier, *The marquise de Belestat*, **1755** (81 x 64cm) [P461]

Nattier's portrait of the marquise de Belestat takes a very different approach. The marquise was a lady-in-waiting to the daughters of Louis XV, including Mesdames Victoire and Marie-Adélaïde. She attended the Court at Versailles in 1754 and 1755. She is shown in the formal *robe à la française*, three-quarter length, without hands and in front of a neutral background. The composition and style of the painting was a formula repeated by Nattier many times for formal portraits of fashionable ladies of the Court. Nattier's objective was to show how closely the sitter's appearance conformed to the current ideals of female beauty rather than to represent her personality.

The Billiard Room

The Arts under Louis XIV and the Régence

The Billiard Room is a showcase for some of the best
furniture by André-Charles Boulle (1642–1732), and
sets the scene for the decorative arts under Louis XIV.
Boulle became cabinet-maker to Louis XIV (1638–1715),
the self-styled Sun King, during whose reign France became pre-eminent in the arts.
The most talented artists of the day, including Boulle, were put to work to promote the
power and magnificence of the monarchy.

c.1890

In 1897, the Billiard Room was dominated by a huge billiard table, now no longer in the
collection. In the nineteenth century most larger houses had a Billiard Room, to which
gentlemen could retire to play this popular game.

André-Charles Boulle, Wardrobe, 1715
(h. 311.5cm) [F429]

The wardrobe is veneered with *contre-partie* Boulle marquetry. The use of metal, mother-of-pearl, horn and precious stones in the decoration of furniture was introduced to France in the 17th century by Italian craftsmen. Boulle developed this technique and gave his name to a type of marquetry using brass and turtleshell in elaborate designs, embellished with gilt-bronze mounts of outstanding quality.

Boulle (1642–1732) was the first great French cabinet-maker. He became cabinet-maker to the King in 1672, on the recommendation of Colbert, the minister of finance. He had lodgings in the Louvre and was thus exempted from guild regulations which forbade cabinet-makers from working in both metal and wood.

To make marquetry, sheets of turtleshell and brass are glued together and the design cut out with a special saw. Once cut, the layers can be combined to produce either a shell ground with a brass design (*première-partie*) or a brass ground with a shell design (*contre-partie*). *Première-partie* cost more than *contre-partie* because turtleshell was more expensive than brass. The brass was often engraved and black pigment rubbed into the engraved lines.

Jean-Marc Nattier *Mademoiselle de Clermont as a Sultana,* **1733**
(109 x 104.5cm) [P456]

Mademoiselle de Clermont is painted as a Sultana taking a bath. Attention is focused on the handsome person of Clermont whose bare legs are placed in the centre of the composition. She is attended by servants and eunuchs. One dries her little foot; another gazes adoringly at her while fingering a string of pearls, a reminder of the pearl-white skin of his mistress. Rich textiles and a sumptuous Turkey carpet add to an atmosphere of lavish exoticism.

Turqueries depict figures in Turkish or oriental dress amidst oriental surroundings. They were the fashion in Paris in the 1720s and 30s, particularly after the visit of the Ottoman Ambassador, Méhémet-Effendi in 1721. Turkish subjects, with their sultans, harems and Turkish baths, licensed a certain wantonness and reflected the dream of a less regulated, luxurious life.

Attributed to André-Charles Boulle, Cabinet-on-stand, *c.*1665–70 (h. 186.7cm) [F16]

This cabinet shows the early development of Boulle's technique. It includes marquetry of exotic woods, which Boulle used at the beginning of his career, and areas of marquetry using metal. The top drawers on each side are veneered with *fleurs-de-lis* and other motifs in pewter, brass and copper against a ground of ebony.[†]

In the Louis XIV period, a cabinet was generally the most elaborate piece of furniture in the house; the term 'cabinet-maker' came to be applied to superior types of joiner from the 1680s. A cabinet consisted of a case of small drawers and compartments intended for the storage and display of precious objects, for example a collection of medals or jewels.

François Lemoyne, *Perseus and Andromeda*, 1723
(183 x 149.7cm) [P417]

The subject of *Perseus and Andromeda* is taken from Ovid's *Metamorphoses*.[†] Andromeda is chained to a rock as a sacrifice to a sea-monster. Her parents and other anguished onlookers stand on the shore in the distance. Perseus, flying overhead, sees the beautiful girl and falls in love. He swoops down to slay the monster and rescue Andromeda. Lemoyne's elegant, colourful style was influenced by Venetian painting and had a profound influence on the development of history painting in 18th-century France. Boucher was one of his pupils.

***Jupiter Victorious over the Titans* and *Juno Controlling the Winds*, after Alessandro Algardi, *c.*1650–89**
(h. 127cm) [S161] (h. 125.8cm) [S162]

Jupiter, seated on his eagle and holding his thunderbolt, represents Fire. Juno, seated on her peacock, symbolises Air. These bronzes derived from models by the Italian sculptor Alessandro Algardi, belonged to the Grand Dauphin, Louis XIV's son. They were amongst the most valuable of over 300 bronzes in the French royal collection.

The Sixteenth-Century Gallery

The Collector's Cabinet

c.1890

The Sixteenth-Century Gallery houses works of art from the Medieval and Renaissance periods and a group of important Renaissance paintings. This part of the Wallace Collection was mainly assembled by Sir Richard who, like many nineteenth-century collectors, was fascinated by the art and history of Europe during the Middle Ages and Renaissance.

The Sixteenth-Century Gallery comprised two smaller rooms during Sir Richard and Lady Wallace's lifetime. The contemporary photograph shows how one room was arranged by Sir Richard as a collector's cabinet, with paintings and maiolica densely hung on the walls and smaller works of art kept in cases or inside Renaissance cabinets. The other room, known as the Canaletto Room (south end), was used to display the collection of paintings by the Venetian artist.

Germain Pilon, *Charles IX*, c.1575 (h. 62.2cm) [S154]

Charles IX was one of France's least distinguished kings. His weak chin and sideways glance in this portrait reveal his vacillating and ineffectual nature. Pilon was one of the greatest French sculptors of the 16th century.

Giovanni Battista Cima da Conegliano, *St Catherine of Alexandria* and *The Virgin and Child with St Francis and St Anthony of Padua*, 1502 (193.2 x 84.9cm) [P1&P1A]

St Catherine stands with a palm leaf, the symbol of Christian martyrdom. The Roman Emperor Maxentius sentenced fifty Christian converts to death and Catherine, herself a convert, tried to intervene on their behalf. Maxentius tried to punish her by tying her to a spiked wheel, but a thunderbolt from heaven destroyed it before it could harm her, so he beheaded her with a sword. You can see a fragment of the wheel behind her. Her iconic status is emphasised by the architectural canopy and the pedestal upon which she stands like a living statue. *St Catherine* originally formed part of an altarpiece in Mestre, near Venice, with the lunette, *The Virgin and Child with St Francis and St Anthony of Padua*, above.

Martial Courteys, *Apollo and the Muses*, c.1580 (w. 56.3cm) [IIIF268]

The platter is a Limoges painted enamel. In the centre, the mythological god Apollo and the nine Muses, goddesses of creative inspiration, make music. Two poets and the winged horse Pegasus are behind them. The nymph in the centre, pouring water from a vase, personifies the castalian spring.

The town of Limoges in France was renowned in the 16th century for its painted enamels. Enamel was fired on to a metal base. Different colours were heated to different temperatures in the kiln and for varying periods of time in order for the components to fuse together to just the right degree. Some of the Muses' dresses have been given an iridescent quality by laying foil under translucent enamel.

Attributed to the Master of Coëtivy, *Boethius instructed by Philosophy, c.1460–70* (24.1 x 16.5cm) [M320]

Illuminated manuscript cuttings are pages from Choir Books and Books of Hours dating from the Middle Ages and the Renaissance. The mutilation of manuscript books for their initials and miniatures was not uncommon in the 18th and 19th centuries.

This is the frontispiece to Book II of a French translation of Boethius' celebrated *On the Consolations of Philosophy*, Boethius listens to Philosophy, in a room covered with tapestry hangings, the windows open to a view of the town. Outside, Fortune turns her wheel: at the top is a king; on the left a prosperous and smug-looking man is on the way up; opposite him another man is on the way down, at the bottom a king falling from the wheel.

Pietro Torrigiano, *Bust of Christ, c.1515* (h. 96.5cm) [S7]

Made for Westminster Abbey, this beautiful marble sculpture by the Florentine artist Pietro Torrigiano (famous for his rivalry with Michelangelo with whom he studied) was among the first artworks in the Italian Renaissance style to be executed in England. He worked for both Henry VII and VIII.

Bowl, Indian, 17th century (w. 16.5cm) [IA16]

This beautiful rock-crystal bowl was made in India during the dynasty of the Mughals, builders of the Taj Mahal. It was later converted to serve as a receptacle for pan (a confection of chopped spiced palm-nuts wrapped in the leaf of a betel tree) by the addition of an exquisite enamelled gold dish and cover.

Goblet, Venetian, *c.1500* (h. 18.0cm) (XXVB92)

This magnificent goblet is an outstanding example of Venetian *calcedonio* glass, made in imitation of the hardstone chalcedony. Complex to make, *calcedonio* exemplifies the technical virtuosity of the Venetian Renaissance glassmakers. They successfully rose to the challenge of imitating nature through art. A contemporary wrote admiringly, '...there is no kind of precious stone which cannot be imitated by the industry of the glassmakers, a sweet contest of man and nature'.

Pieter Pourbus, *An Allegory of True Love*, c.1547
(132.8 x 205.7cm) [P531]

In *An Allegory of True Love,* a winged Cupid, on the left, and
a Jester, on the right, warn of the folly of carnal love. In the
centre, Wisdom embraces Fidelity, who points at the table
laden with the food of love. The other mythological and
allegorical characters are arranged in four groups of three,
each consisting of a famous classical lover embracing one
of the Graces but distracted by a female figure symbolising,
from left to right, inconstancy, superficial emotion,
fickleness, and luxury and excess.

Standing salt and cover, London, 1578
(h. 30.6cm) [XIIA104]

The silver-gilt† standing salt was made in Elizabethan
London. Salt was kept beneath the cover on a recess
at the top of the main drum. The decoration was made
by hammering the silver from the back and then chasing
the surface.

Salt was a rare, necessary and valuable commodity in
the Renaissance. Table wares for salt ('salts') became
ceremonial objects whose size was out of all proportion
to the small amount of salt which they contained. A
salt was used to mark the place of the highest-ranking
person at the table.

Lucas Horenbout, *Portrait of Holbein*, 1543
(4.2 x 4.2cm) [M203]

The *Portrait of Holbein* is
painted on vellum† laid
on a 16th-century playing
card; two hearts are just
visible. Horenbout, a leading
miniaturist of the Ghent-
Bruges school, was appointed
King's Painter to Henry VIII of
England in 1534. In his service
he became the friend and
teacher of Hans Holbein, who
is shown painting with a paint
pot in his left hand.

The Oriental Armoury

The extremely fine Indian, Persian, Turkish, Balkan and Arab weapons and armour displayed in this gallery represent one of the best such collections in Britain. Unlike the European arms and armour, which was acquired by Sir Richard Wallace, the Oriental material was collected by the 4th Marquess of Hertford, mostly in the last decade of his life, between 1860 and 1870.

*c.*1890

This space was originally the bedroom and sitting room of Sir Richard and Lady Wallace's butler. The Oriental arms and armour was displayed on the first floor, in what is now the East Galleries and Drawing Room. Like the European arms displays that once filled the current Nineteenth-Century Gallery, this part of the collection was mounted in dense trophy groupings extending almost to the ceiling, which was itself painted a deep blue and decorated with golden stars.

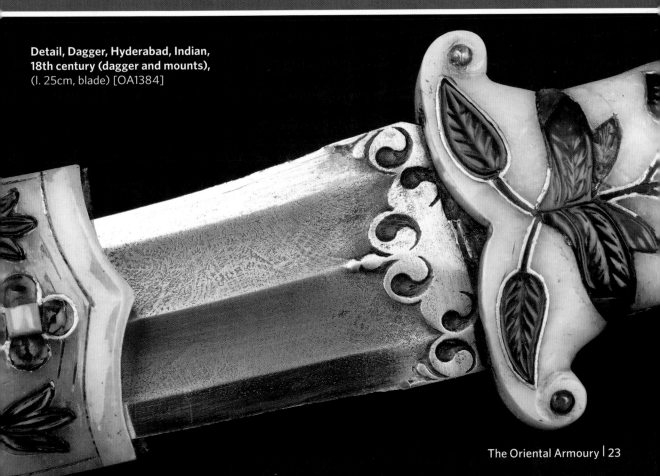

Detail, Dagger, Hyderabad, Indian, 18th century (dagger and mounts), (l. 25cm, blade) [OA1384]

Dagger (*chilanum*), Indian, early 17th century
(l. 36cm) [OA1409]

This north Indian dagger is without question one of the finest in the world. It might have been made for a very high-ranking nobleman at the court of the Mughal Emperor in India. It could even have been made for one of the Mughal Emperors themselves, perhaps Jahangir, the son of Akbar the Great (reigned 1556–1605), or his son Shah Jahan (reigned 1632–47), builder of the Taj Mahal. Indeed a portrait survives of Shah Jahan, in which he is wearing a dagger exactly like this one, the knuckle-guard terminating in a duck's head.

The dagger hilt is made of solid gold, with very dense settings, of diamonds, rubies and emeralds, some cut so small that they are little more than slivers, forming intricate floral patterns.

Dagger, Iran, 1496–7 (l. 34cm) [OA1414]

This Persian dagger is one of the earliest and most beautiful of its kind known to exist. The carved jade hilt is inlaid with gold, while the blade is exquisitely carved and gilt with jackals, hares, lotus flowers and arabesques in relief. The blade is also signed and dated, making it especially significant.

Sword (*tulwar*) of Tipu Sultan, Indian, late 18th century
(l. 89cm) [OA1402]

Other weapons in the Oriental collection can be more firmly connected with famous historical figures. The blade of this fine *tulwar* is inscribed in gold 'the personal sword of Tipu Sultan'. Tipu was ruler of the sovereign kingdom of Mysore in south India at the end of the 18th century. He was killed by British troops at the Siege of Seringapathan in 1799.

The hilt of Tipu's sword was carved from a single chunk of cloudy jade and inlaid with gold, rubies and emeralds.

The Oriental collection includes a number of objects associated with the Sikh Kingdoms in the Punjab. Although it is often impossible to determine whether or not a weapon is of Sikh origin in particular (Sikh warriors used weapons from all over India), certain pieces in this collection have strong Sikh associations.

Sword (*shamshir*), associated with Ranjit Singh, Indian, early 19th century (l. 92cm) [OA1404]

Most iconic of all the Indian swords in the Wallace Collection is this exceptionally rich sword, said to have belonged to Ranjit Singh, founder of the Sikh dynasty in what is now the Province of Punjab in Pakistan. The ivory grip is joined to a pommel and guard of solid gold, carved with bulls' heads. The top of the grip is fitted with a velvet lanyard embroidered with tiny seed pearls and coloured stones. The exquisite blade is made of 'watered' steel: the carbon content of the metal has been manipulated to produce a magical rippling pattern when lightly-etched with a weak acid.

Helmet, Indian, late 18th century (h. 37.4cm) [OA1769]

Another piece that can be definitely identified as being distinctively Sikh is this fine helmet, inlaid with scrolling foliage and hung with a mail aventail protecting the sides of the head and shoulders. The steel skull is embossed to accommodate the characteristically Sikh *jooda* (hair topknot).

Shield (*dhal*), Indian, early 19th century (w. 42cm) [OA2188]

Similarly, this shield can be identified as a Sikh object from the portraits and names of important Sikh figures that fill the inlaid gold border. Above this border are lively hunting scenes, in which warriors slay lions, antelope and hares with spears, swords, bows and firearms.

The 4th Marquess of Hertford collected 'Orientalist' paintings as well as arms and armour. His taste for Oriental material was typical of his time, when increased British activity in India and the Middle East, combined with Napoleon's invasion of Egypt in 1798, had stimulated European interest in the art and material culture of Turkey, Arabia, Persia and India.

Alexandre-Gabriel Decamps, *The Punishment of the Hooks*, 1837 (99 x 135.5cm) [P345]

Alexandre-Gabriel Decamps (1803–60) visited the Middle East in 1828, and thus became the first major French artist to focus on Orientalist subjects. *The Punishment of the Hooks* is characteristic of a particular vein of Orientalist painting – depictions of barbaric customs of a sort no longer practiced in western Europe.

Horace Vernet, *The Arab Tale-Teller*, 1833 (99 x 136.5cm) [P280]

Vernet painted *The Arab Tale-Teller* after his first visit to Algeria in 1833. A group of men sit in the shade of a fig tree to escape the midday sun. They smoke and listen to a story told by the man in a grey and white striped robe, who sits on an oriental carpet. In the background are the tents, horses and livestock of the nomads. A girl resembling a Classical statue stands with an urn on her shoulder. European artists had a romantic admiration for the lives of North African and Middle Eastern peoples, which they regarded as unchanged since the time of Christ.

Full armour, Indian, late-18th century
[OA1790–94, OA1828]

This impressive armour was made for a wealthy Rajput warrior. The Rajputs were a martial culture from north-western India; they were comparable in many ways to the knights of medieval Europe. The main structure of this armour is made of layers of fabric studded with thousands of copper alloy nails. Additional reinforcement is provided by plates of watered steel, damascened in gold. The arm defences (*dastána*) and helmet (*tóp*) are decorated in a similar manner. A fine sword (*khanda*) hangs from a tablet-woven baldrick.

The European Armoury I

The arms and armour, horse equipment and cutlery, displayed in the first room of the European Armouries date from primarily the fourteenth to the early-sixteenth centuries. Sir Richard Wallace acquired almost all of his arms, armour and related material in one year, 1871. In this year he bought the collection of his friend Alfred Émilien, comte de Nieuwerkerke, Minister of Fine Arts to Napoleon III and Director of the Louvre, as well as parts of the once much larger collection of Sir Samuel Rush Meyrick, one of the fathers of the modern scholarly study of arms and armour.

Armour displays on the first floor, *c.*1890

In Sir Richard Wallace's time the collection of European arms and armour was displayed in a single massive arrangement upstairs, in what is now the Nineteenth-Century Gallery.

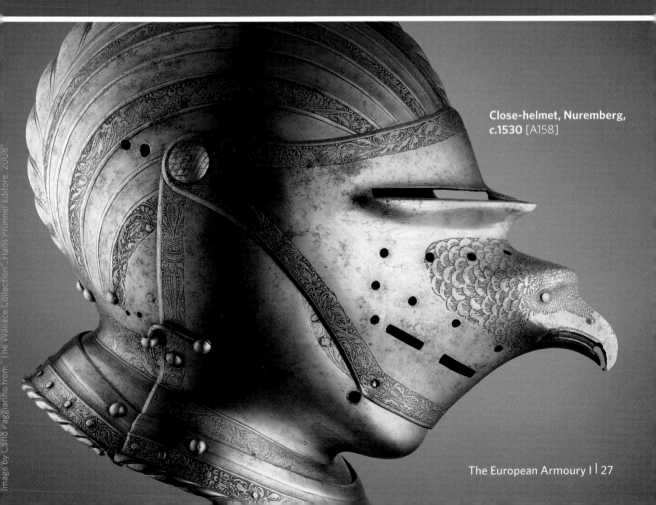

Close-helmet, Nuremberg, *c.*1530 [A158]

Visored bascinet, Milanese, c.1380–1410
(h. 37.4cm) [A69]

The visored bascinet is one of the most iconic helmets of the late Middle Ages. Helmets in this style were worn by knights and men-at-arms all over Europe in the late-14th and early-15th centuries.

The skull of this one is older than the visor: when the skull was first made, in around 1380, it was fitted with a small visor pivoted centrally on the brow. The old attachment hole on the forehead is now filled with a rivet. Later in the helmet's working lifetime, the original visor was replaced with the later style pivoted at the sides. The visor has been drawn out with great skill to form the snouted shape fashionable at the time. Such visors were excellent protection, particularly against arrows.

The full armours worn on late medieval and Renaissance battlefields was generally much lighter than is often imagined today. Typically, a full war armour was around half the weight of the campaign packs carried by most modern soldiers. The weight of an armour was distributed over the whole body, and the fit was tailored so that no one part of the body was bearing an uncomfortable load.

Composite field armour, South German, c.1475–1510 [A20]

Although this armour is composite – made up of parts originally made for several different armours – it gives a good general impression of a German war 'harness' of the late-15th and early-16th centuries. The plates are drawn out into sharp points in many places, and their main surfaces are embossed with sharp ridges or flutes: a simple but very graceful form of decoration. To maximise the wearer's mobility, plate protection for the shoulders and arms has been kept to a minimum, with secondary protection provided by a mail shirt worn under the plates. Mail (it should never be called 'chain-mail') was an art in itself, a cloth of iron formed of tens of thousands of tiny metal links.

Sallet, in the so-called 'Corinthian' style, Milanese, c.1450–60 (h. 27.5 cm) [A75]

The graceful lines and proportions of this fine Italian helmet are a proud reminder that, for the people that made and used it, armour was an art-form as well as protective equipment. The smooth, rounded surfaces are as aesthetically pleasing as any abstract sculpture. The form of this particular example was probably inspired by the helmets of the Ancient Greeks; it forms a direct visual connection between the Renaissance warrior who wore it and the heroes of Classical antiquity.

Kolman Helmschmid, Parade helmet, c.1520 [A105]

This parade helmet is a rich and expensive costume piece. The finely-polished skull has been embossed with lines of thick roping along the lower edge and a large scallop shell at the back. Separate embossed, blued and gilt plates, forming a pair of wings at the sides and a grotesque, double-tailed dolphin over the brow, have then been attached by means of a system of turn-pins.

Sallet, probably Nuremberg, c.1500–10 (w. 23cm) [A82]

As well as often displaying beauty of form, armour was also an obvious surface onto which many different kinds of decoration could be applied. Plate armour was often painted, though very few intact examples survive today. Paint was a relatively inexpensive way by which cheaper, lower quality armour could be made to look much more impressive. This German sallet of the early-16th century retains its complete painted surface, the visor emblazoned with a tusked, monstrous face.

Paint was the least expensive form of armour decoration. For those who had money, there were much more elaborate possibilities. A smooth, mirror-bright surface was a powerful sign of status, since fine polishing was difficult and very expensive. Polished steel could then be given an iridescent blue-purple tint by heating it very carefully. For their wealthiest patrons, armourers could also cover their work in gold, by means of fire-gilding.

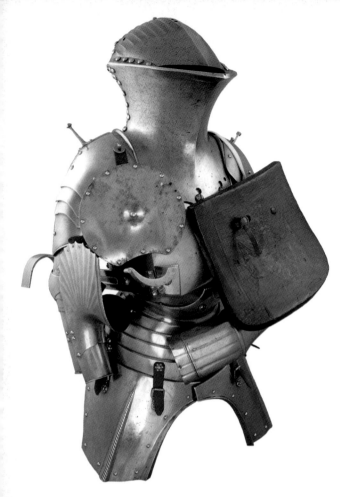

Arms and armour were used for much more than warfare. Jousts and tournaments played an important part in a knight's life. These were controlled martial contests or combat sports, in which knights could display their riding and fighting abilities in a friendly, festive environment. Jousts 'of peace' were held to celebrate great social or political events, such as marriages or treaties. They required specially – designed safety equipment such as a heavy jousting helm and shield. These pieces, much thicker than anything worn on the battlefield, were guaranteed to protect the jouster in friendly contests where it was important that no one was seriously hurt.

Composite armour for the German joust of peace or *Gestech*, Nuremberg, *c.*1500–20 [A23]

This jousting armour is nearly twice the weight of a war armour of the same period. However, it was, only meant to be worn for short periods of time, in a controlled situation. The use of armours such as this was not well understood in the 19th century. This lack of understanding may have contributed to the grossly incorrect modern conception of the lumbering knight imprisoned in his over-heavy armour, unable to mount his horse or recover if knocked to the ground.

Crossbow, German, *c.*1450–75 (l. 72cm) [A1032]

Hunting was another essential aristocratic activity. The hunting weapons of noblemen were usually decorated, often in much more elaborate ways than their battlefield counterparts. The crossbow was one of the most common hunting weapons; the stock of this crossbow, one of the finest medieval examples in existence, is entirely sheathed in horn plaques with scenes finely carved in relief.

Falchion[†] of Cosimo de' Medici, Grand Duke of Tuscany, North Italian, 1546–9 (l. 61cm) [A710]

Weapons, like armour, could be used to express ideas and form visual associations. This exceptionally fine short-sword or 'falchion', having a wide, cleaver-like blade, may be a fiercesome weapon but it is also a statement. It was designed to look like the sword of a Classical hero, and was probably worn with a parade costume in the Roman or *all 'antica'* style. Renaissance nobleman, especially in Italy, routinely dressed in the 'heroic' fashion for parades, ceremonies, and other special occasions. This sword was probably part of such an impressive costume, intended to create the idea that its owner was the heir to an ancient line of heroes.

The European Armoury II

The displays in this gallery contain some of the finest mid-to-late-sixteenth-century arms and armour in the collection: the princely weapons and armour of emperors, kings and princes, worn for war, jousts, tournaments and parades.

This room did not exist in Sir Richard Wallace's time. The space was originally part of the central stableyard, with the stables themselves being located at the west side of the present gallery.

Armour displays on the first floor, c.1890

Rooms II and III of the European Armoury were created when Hertford House was converted into a museum between 1897 and 1900. The European arms and armour was moved to this location from its original display space on the first floor, in what is now the Nineteenth-Century Gallery.

Parts of a parade armour, probably by Lucio Marliani, called Piccinino, *c.*1570–90 (weight 10.9kg) [A51]

Armour for man and horse, Nuremberg, *c.*1532–6
(weight 54.87kg) [A29]

The impressive armour of the Elector Otto Heinrich, Count Palatine of the Rhine, often called 'Ottheinrich', is actually composed of parts of several black and gold armours made for this famous South German nobleman by the Nuremberg master Hans Ringler between 1532 and 1536.

Ottheinrich was an early champion of the Protestant faith, and went to war with the Emperor Charles V to defend it, commanding his forces in support of the Protestant alliance against the Emperor in the War of Schmalkalden (1546–7). Ottheinrich was a lavish patron of the arts and has been called 'the German Henry VIII' who in many ways he resembled.

Armour for man and horse, South German, *c.*1480–1500 (weight 37.33kg) [A21]

This famous equestrian armour, one of only two in Britain, once belonged to a lord of the Freyberg family of Hohenaschau Castle in South Germany.

Although partly composite with a number of 19th-century restorations, this armour is historically very important. The horse armour is nearly complete and thus extremely rare. The horse's face-guard or 'shaffron' bears the city mark of Landshut as well as an armourer's mark, in the form of an 'R', which has been ascribed to the master Ulrich Rämbs. Other parts of the armour were probably also made in Landshut.

Garniture for the field, made under royal licence granted to Sir Thomas Sackville, Lord Buckhurst, Greenwich, *c.*1587 (weight 32.02kg) [A62]

This fabulous war armour was made in about 1587 at the Royal workshops at Greenwich, established by Henry VIII in the 1520s. The form of the armour mirrors Elizabethan civilian dress. For example, the shape of the breastplate mirrors the form of contemporary 'peascod' doublets.

The Greenwich style combined simple basic construction with stupendous decoration, especially very rich etching and gilding. The plain areas of this armour were also heat-tinted to a deep blue-purple hue, traces of which colour can still be seen.

The armour includes exchange pieces that were used to configure it variously for light, medium and heavy cavalry combat.

Field armour, South German, *c.*1515–25 (weight 18.99kg) [A24]

The so-called 'Maximilian' style is named after the German Emperor Maximilian I, under whose patronage it was developed. This armour is a typical example of the style, which is characterised by the dense groups of straight radiating flutes that cover all parts of the body except the lower legs. The flutes echo the folds and pleats fashionable in the civilian dress of the early-16th century, while the plain greaves recall the contemporary fashion for the calves to be shown off, clad only in closely-fitted stockings.

The very narrow waist was another important fashionable detail. Here the waist has been made as narrow as possible, while its smallness is further exaggerated by the deep, round chest and the straight, boldly roped upper edge of the breastplate.

Kolman Helmschmid and Daniel Hopfer, partial armour, c.1525–30 (weight 16.3kg) [A30]

This now incomplete armour was almost certainly made by Kolman Helmschmid, court armourer to Charles V, German Emperor and King of Spain, the grandson of Maximilian I. Although it is very elaborately decorated with etching, embossing, gilding and filework, many of the main surfaces have been left purposefully plain, so that both aesthetic qualities of the armour, its pure sculptural forms and the rich decoration, could be appreciated together, in perfect harmony. It is possible that Charles V commissioned this armour as a present for his younger brother Ferdinand, who would later succeed him as Emperor.

Like his older brother, Ferdinand was a great patron of the armourer's art. In 1555 he had four 'golden garnitures' made for himself and his three sons – the future Emperor Maximilian II, the Archduke Ferdinand II of Tyrol, and Archduke Charles II of Styria.

All great Renaissance men had to have the finest arms and armour that money could buy. The wealthiest nobles – emperors, kings and princes – employed the very best armourers at their courts. The role of a court armourer was to make metal masterpieces for his lord to wear in war, jousts, tournaments, and important ceremonies and parades.

Close helmet for tournament combat on foot, Augsburg, c.1555 (weight 5.62kg) [A188]

These armours were fabulously decorated with gilding and etching over their whole surface. This helmet is one of only a very few pieces from this series known to survive. Although this armour was incredibly rich and expensive, it was still used in combat – the front is marked by many hard sword blows.

Parts of a parade armour, probably by Lucio Marliani, called Piccinino, c.1570–90 (weight 10.9kg) [A51]

Although most of the richly decorated armour in the Wallace Collection was intended for combat, either on the battlefield or in jousts and tournaments, a few of the most ornate pieces are purely a breed of wearable art, intricately sculpted steel costumes covered in precious metal.

The best example of such costume armour is this magnificent work, an awe-inspiring demonstration of metalworking genius. The entire surface is covered in very dense and diverse motifs, including Hercules and the Nemean Lion, Roman soldiers and mythical beasts, all contained in rich strapwork bands set against a background of silver cartouches and tiny, twisting arabesques. There is an old tradition that it was made for Alfonso II d'Este, Duke of Ferrara, a great patron of the arts in late-16th-century Italy.

The European Armoury III

The arms and armour in the European Armoury III, range from the sixteenth to the nineteenth centuries. The array of smooth-bore long guns, rifles and pistols, including magnificent weapons made for the kings of France and flint-lock sporting guns of the Napoleonic era, constitutes one of the finest collections of early firearms in the United Kingdom.

Like Gallery II of the European Armoury, this room was created for the museum between 1897 and 1900, over what was once the stables and coach house.

Armour displays on the first floor, *c.*1890

Detail, Wheel-lock pistol with ramrod, German, *c.*1610 (l. 57.4cm) [A1154]

Wheel-lock gun, from the armoury of King Louis XIII of France, French, *c.*1620 (l. 132cm) [A1111]

A number of the finest firearms in the Wallace Collection are of French manufacture, with several being directly associated with the French crown. Most of the royal weapons, not surprisingly, are extremely elaborate in terms of their decoration. However, one could be forgiven for at first glance overlooking this rather plain long gun, which is in fact one of the personal guns of King Louis XIII. Although it is not covered in gold and intricate carving, this wheel-lock gun is exceptionally well-made, the smooth, sharp lines of the stock flowing around the lock and extending to support the long barrel. This work is a reminder that even as late as the 17th century, when the ostentatious Rococo style was coming to dominate, the old idea of beauty that is derived from simplicity, from perfection of form and line, was still valued.

Detail, pair of flint-lock pistols of King Louis XIV of France, French, *c.*1660 (l. 59.7cm) [A1209–10]

This extraordinary pair of pistols were made for King Louis XIV of France. They are of the very highest quality, the faceted barrels heat-blued and damascened in gold with fleurs-de-lis, the French royal device. The dark walnut stocks are carved in high relief with depictions of Hercules and the Nemean Lion and Samson slaughtering the Philistines. Each pistol carries an inscription that presents Hercules as a personification of France. The war-like themes and inscriptions indicate that these weapons were made to commemorate a military success, probably the French victory over the Spanish at the Battle of the Dunes (1658). The makers of these lavish objects remain unidentified. Art works made for royalty were usually unsigned, and so it is not surprising that these weapons have been left devoid of makers' marks.

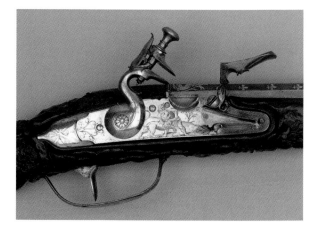

Before the 16th century swords were rarely worn with everyday dress, but by the mid-1500s, they had become indispensable fashion accessories. Rapiers, that is, swords intended specifically for use in civilian life, were elaborately decorated according to the means and social status of the owner. Rapier hilts are exceptionally interesting as demonstrations of fine Renaissance metalwork. Their creation involved many different ornamental techniques, with the best work combining several forms of expensive decoration.

The rapiers in the Wallace Collection exhibit the full range of decorative options available in the 16th and 17th centuries. These include inlay and encrusting in gold and/or silver, heat bluing, fire-gilding, steel carving and chiselling, engraving, piercing and file-work.

Just like the flamboyant clothing that they were designed to accompany, rapiers varied in style of region to region. Italian and Spanish examples often have hilts made up of delicate, narrow bars and proportionately restrained pommels. This fineness is further enhanced through the use of refined, elegant ornamentation, especially minute relief carving and damascening. English rapiers, in contrast, tend to have a burlier, more robust quality, with large, round pommels and bold, silver-encrusted guards.

Rapier, English, blade German, *c.*1605–15
(l. 113.4cm) [A596]

Rapier, Spanish, *c.*1585–1600
(l. 104.7cm) [A611]

Rapier, Italian, blade Spanish, *c.*1585–1620
(l. 102.2cm) [A609]

Two priming flasks, Spanish, c.1555
(each weigh 0.19kg) [A1295–6]

Most early firearms were accompanied by a set of tools and accessories, such as these priming flasks. Priming flasks carried a small amount of gunpowder for filling the pan (or 'priming') of a wheel-lock gun. This mini-charge was set off by the sparks struck by the lock's flint when the trigger was pulled, in turn igniting the main charge and firing the weapon.

Some firearms accessories were little works of art in themselves, as elaborate as the weapons to which they belonged. These two flasks are each decorated with a scene from Roman history, delicately cast in sharp relief.

Wheel-lock gun, Munich, c.1620
(l. 170cm) [A1090]

This wheel-lock gun was made for a member of the Bavarian Electoral Court in Munich by the celebrated Sadelar family of metalworkers and the gunstock master Hieronymus Borstorffer. The stock and barrel are richly gilded and chiselled in relief with Classical figures including Bacchus, god of wine, and Diana, goddess of the hunt. This piece was once part of the extensive personal collection of Napoleon III of France.

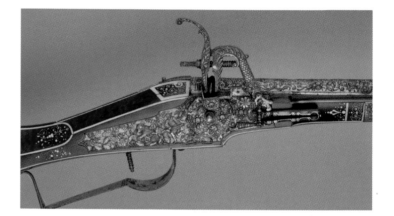

Nicolas-Noël Boutet, cased double-barrelled flint-lock rifle, tools and accessories of Tsar Nicholas I of Russia, c.1805 (l. 102cm) [A1126]

The Landing

The Landing still looks much as it did in Sir Richard Wallace's day and serves as the main orientation point on the first floor. It is hung with an outstanding group of mythological and pastoral paintings by François Boucher, the leading French painter of the middle of the eighteenth century, and is also perhaps the best place to admire the stunning wrought iron work of the staircase balustrade, made in 1719 for the Royal Bank in Paris.

*c.*1890

François Boucher, *The Setting of the Sun*, 1752
(318 x 261cm) [P486]

Every day Apollo, the sun god, rises from the river Oceanus, which surrounds the earth, and drives his chariot across the heavens bringing light to the world. In the evening he sinks back beneath the waves where he is attended by the nymph, Tethys, and the sons and daughters of the sea.

In *The Setting of the Sun*, Apollo has completed his journey and dismounts from his chariot into the open arms of Tethys. Far above him shines the Evening Star and winged infants pull across the dark clouds of night.

Madame de Pompadour, Louis XV's mistress, ordered tapestries based on Boucher's paintings and both paintings and tapestries at one time hung in her château at Bellevue. The scenes derive from Ovid's *Metamorphoses*.[†] Madame de Pompadour was clearly involved in the choice of iconography for the paintings, casting herself in the role of Tethys welcoming home Louis XV after a hard day with affairs of state.

François Boucher, *The Rising of the Sun*, 1753
(318 x 261cm) [P485]

In *The Rising of the Sun*, Apollo prepares for his journey across the sky while Tethys holds the reins of his white horses. Meanwhile Aurora, goddess of the dawn, sets out to scatter her pink roses across the sky. She is crowned by the Morning Star and behind her winged infants push back the clouds of the night.

The Rising and *The Setting of the Sun* incurred fierce criticism at the 1753 Salon.[†] One commentator complained that their excessive nudity was so shocking that one should not take one's wife or daughter to the Salon.

Evacuation of the collection, August, 1939

Hertford House narrowly escaped destruction in the Blitz of World War II. In the courtyard floor you can see a paving stone which flew over the roof in 1940. Fortunately the collection had already been evacuated.

François Boucher, *A Summer Pastoral*, 1749
(259 x 197cm) [P482]

The paintings depict characters from Charles-Simon Favart's pantomimes, which combine the sensibilities of pastoral poetry with the rustic characters of popular theatre. *Summer* shows the cousins Babette and Lisette with the Little Shepherd. He serenades his sweetheart,

Lisette, on the musette (bagpipes) to win the crown of flowers held at her side.

François Boucher, *An Autumn Pastoral*, 1749
(259 x 197cm) [P489]

Autumn depicts a scene from a pantomime first performed in 1745; the Little Shepherd feeds grapes to the heroine, Lisette. Boucher designed theatre sets for his friend, Favart.

Staircase balustrade, 1719–20 [F68]

The staircase balustrade is made from cast and wrought iron and gilt-brass.† A heart-shaped cartouche frames the interlaced 'L's of Louis XV. If you trace the S and C-shaped scrolls you will find sunflowers, a reference to the King. Horns of plenty overflow with fruit, coins and banknotes, a reference to the wealth promised by

France's new banking system and speculation in shares. The balustrade was commissioned for a building in Paris which in 1719 was destined to become the Royal Bank. However, a year later the entire financial system crashed and five years after that, the building became the King's Library. Bought by Richard Wallace, the balustrade was altered to fit Hertford House and installed in 1874.

The Small Drawing Room

c.1890

The Early Rococo

The room is furnished to celebrate the rococo style of the *fête galante* and the passion for Chinese works of art in early-eighteenth-century France. The paintings by Watteau and his followers in the Wallace Collection form one of the most important groups in existence. As Louis XIV's reign waned there was a new lightness of touch at court. The Italian *Commedia dell'arte* players returned to France, having been banished by Louis XIV. Their exotic costumes and theatrical characters represent the new freedom and spirit of the age. They can be seen in this room not only in pictures, but in sculpture, a clock and the Meißen ewers.

In Sir Richard Wallace's day this room was known as the Reynolds Drawing Room. In it hung most of the superb group of paintings by Sir Joshua Reynolds in the Wallace Collection.

Jean-Antoine Watteau, *The Music Party, c.1718/9*
(67.3 x94.8cm) [P410]

In *The Music Party,* a woman plays the guitar on a palatial terrace; a man leans against her chair. In the centre another man tunes a large lute in preparation for making love to the seated lady by playing and singing to her. But it takes a long time to tune his lute. Watteau was fascinated by such moments of emotional suspense.

Watteau (1684–1721) gave expression to a new atmosphere in early 18th-century Paris. His synthesis of Rubensian colour and naturalistic observation fitted perfectly the new taste for small and intimate works suitable for the less formal rooms of the period. His elegant and amorous outdoor companies, or *fêtes galantes,* were a fresh genre in Paris giving a visual form to contemporary ideals of sociability. Watteau delighted in *commedia dell'arte,* the ribald comedy of carnival tradition which started as a popular entertainment in early 16th-century Italy. Its stock characters, including Harlequin, Columbine and Mezzetin, take part in absurd and witty plots wearing costumes and masks. Watteau happily mixed theatrical and contemporary costumes. His critics correctly pointed out that he painted pictures with no easily identifiable subject.

Jean-Antoine Watteau, *Harlequin and Columbine*, *c*.1715/6 (36 x 24.9cm) [P387]

Harlequin and Columbine shows Columbine recoiling from Harlequin's advances. Behind them a guitarist plays and a seated couple follow a musical score. The *commedia dell'arte* characters Pierrot and Crispin are in the background. Harlequin's inopportune love-making is expressed by his demoniac emergence from the shadows and his awkward lunge.

Jean-Antoine Watteau, *Gilles and his Family*, *c*.1716–8 (27.1 x 19cm) [P381]

In *Gilles and his Family*, the central figure is dressed in the costume of the *commedia dell'arte* character, Mezzetin, the rascally valet, musician and rival of Harlequin. His libidinous character is suggested by the sculpted faun above his head.

Nicholas-Jean Marchand, Commode (chest-of-drawers), 1755 (h. 84.5cm) [F88]

The commode is one of a pair delivered to the French royal palace of Fontainebleau for the bedroom of Queen Marie Leczinska, wife of Louis XV. It is veneered with panels of Chinese lacquer in a way which ignores the logic of the pictorial decoration on the lacquer, a common occurrence in French 18th-century furniture making. Notice how the gilt-bronze† mounts incorporate drawer handles.

Antoine-Nicolas Martinière, Perpetual almanac, 1741–2
(h. 46cm) [F64 & F65]

The capacity of the perpetual almanac to predict the exact order of time for eternity would have seemed quite magical when it was made for Louis XV by the enameller, Martinière. The twelve months are split between four gilt-bronze frames which bear dedications to the King. Each month has three columns containing plaques, made of copper, on which are painted in enamel the phases of the moon, the days of the week, the dates, the month, the nearest sign of the Zodiac and the Saints' days and feast and fast days of the Church. The frames have removable brass backs so that the plaques can be adjusted at the end of the year.

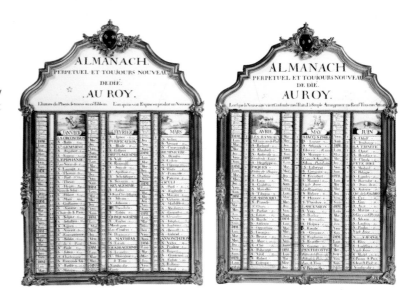

Workshop of Jean-François Oeben, Toilet and writing-table, c.1763–4
(h. 70.8cm) [F110]

The toilet and writing-table would have been used by a lady to make her toilette and write her morning letters. The compartments were for writing materials, scent bottles, pomade pots, brushes and so on. It was made in the workshop of

Chinese lacquer starts life as the sap of the *rhus vernicifera* tree, a grey syrupy juice which becomes plastic on exposure to air. It is applied to a material such as wood in numerous very thin layers, each of which must dry before the next coat is added. Here the lacquer is dyed black and decorated with gilding and coloured lacquer.

Oeben and shows the mechanical ingenuity which he introduced into late Louis XV furniture.

The marquetry table top depicts a naturalistic basket of flowers, assembled from many pieces of veneer, engraved to show the veining of the leaves and petals.

The East Drawing Room

c.1890

During the refurbishment of the adjacent East Galleries the East Drawing Room shows selected masterworks of Netherlandish seventeenth-century painting – both Dutch and Flemish – in the Wallace Collection. The towering figure of the first decades of the century was Peter Paul Rubens who worked in Antwerp in Flanders for a wide international clientele. A generation later, Dutch art had become the leading force in the Netherlands. Rembrandt and his workshop developed a new, regional variant of the international baroque style which was based in Italian and Flemish models. In the further course of the century, Dutch painting became known for its brilliant sense of observation, its successful staging of reality and its high degree of specialization.

In Sir Richard Wallace's day, this room was mainly hung with Dutch pictures. In the first decades of the nineteenth century, the East Drawing Room was Isabella, Marchioness of Hertford's sitting room. Here she entertained the Prince Regent during his daily visits which lasted throughout their liaison, from 1807 until his accession as George IV in 1820. At the time the room was furnished with salmon coloured silk curtains, white and gold seat furniture and Isabella's collection of Sèvres porcelain.

Jan Steen, *Celebrating the Birth*, 1664
(87.7 x 107cm) [P111]

In 17th-century Holland the birth of a baby was celebrated with a party. This was supposed to be a sober affair but gatherings often became riotous and legislation was introduced to control them. *Celebrating the Birth* (overleaf) is one such riot. The mother lies in bed at the top left corner of the painting; the apparent father holds the baby, wrapped in a red cloth. Another man, a self-portrait of Jan Steen, makes the sign of cuckold's horns behind the baby's head. The cuckold is further emasculated by the apron, keys and purse strings around his waist (domestic duties should be carried out by the mistress of the house).

Caspar Netscher, *The Lace Maker*, 1662
(33 x 27cm) [P237]

The Lace Maker carries the opposite message to the painting by Jan Steen. It says, 'Do behave like this!' A young woman sits in an immaculate interior. In Dutch 17th-century opinion, a woman was easily corrupted if left to her own devices. The home was the bedrock of the new Dutch republic and a corrupt wife meant a corrupt home which in turn could wreak havoc on society. Many tracts and manuals instructed women and their husbands on correct use of female time.

Gerard ter Borch, *A Lady Reading a Letter*, early 1660s
(44.2 x 32.2cm) [P236]

A Lady Reading a Letter shows a woman sitting at a table reading a love letter. The carpet covering the table has been pushed aside for sewing, but the woman's work lies unattended in a basket at her side. The painting has a curious stillness, like a rain drop suspended in mid-air for a fraction of a second. While she studies her lover's words, we can study the girl, her earring, the curl of her hair, but not her thoughts.

Rembrandt van Rijn, *Self-Portrait in a Black Cap, c.*1637 (63 x 50.7cm) [P52]

This painting has recently been reattributed to Rembrandt. It is a powerful and entirely effective self portrait, in keeping with his more vigorous style of the second half of the 1630s. The unusual semi-circular shape was due to the oak panel probably being cut down to fit a particular location. This must have been done before 1837 when the painting was first described.

Govaert Flinck, *A Young Archer, c.*1639–40 (66.2 x 50.8cm) [P238]

Tronies are character studies of heads in exotic dress, a genre developed by Rembrandt and Jan Lievens in their Leiden studio, 1626–31. The Young Archer may be a *tronie* or he may be a specific character; the same subject appears in a print by Jan de Visscher with an inscription, 'Thus the Moor with bow and arrow has the foe or the game in sight'.

Pieter de Hooch, *A Boy Bringing Bread*, c.1660–3
(73.5 x 59cm) [P27]

A Boy Bringing Bread shows the physical meeting of public and domestic worlds. The housewife receives the boy who brings bread. Beyond them, through the open doorway, areas of public and private space are indicated with bands of light and shadow: first, the courtyard of the house, then the outer passage, the pavement, the canal, the pavement on the other side of the canal and another private house with a woman standing at the door.

Peter Paul Rubens,
***The Birth of Henri IV*, 1628**
(21.5 x 37.2cm) [P523]

Peter Paul Rubens,
***The Union of Henri IV and Marie de Médicis*, 1628**
(23 x 12.2cm) [P524]

The Birth and *The Union* (and *The Triumph of Henri IV*, also in this gallery) belong to a set of *modelli* prepared by Rubens for a series of twenty-four paintings, *The Life of Henri IV*. The series was commissioned by Marie de Médicis, the widow of Henri IV, King of France (a series celebrating and glorifying Marie de Médicis' life had already been painted by Rubens.) Work on the full-size paintings was abandoned when Marie de Médicis fell out with her son, Louis XIII. She was exiled from France by Cardinal Richelieu in 1631.

Rubens' modelli were oil sketch designs for paintings. Assistants in Rubens' large Antwerp studio worked up the full-size painting from the modello. The degree of Rubens' participation varied from commission to commission, sometimes the whole painting, sometimes just finishing hands and faces – and customers were charged accordingly. Rubens' modelli are highly valued as the true work of the master's hand, showing the spontaneity of his thought processes as he drew with paint.

Jan van der Heyden, *View of the Westerkerk, Amsterdam*, 1667/8–72 (41.3 x 59.1cm) [P225]

The paintings by Van der Heyden demonstrate the Dutchman's delight in celebrating what he saw with his eyes by describing it in paint. The Westerkerk, built 1620-1, is viewed from across the Keizersgracht in Amsterdam. The detail on the façade of the church and its reflection in the canal are magical. You can see every brick on the canal wall.

The Large Drawing Room

Monumental French furniture

In Sir Richard Wallace's lifetime, the Large Drawing Room was then, as now, dominated by monumental Boulle furniture, including the enormous Londonderry Bookcase, and large Dutch paintings. These powerful works of art within a darkly masculine setting evoke one strand of taste among collectors in eighteenth-century France.

c.1890

In the early nineteenth century, this room and the adjoining Oval Drawing Room were ballrooms. The 2nd Marchioness was famous for the sumptuous dinners, receptions and balls which she gave, including in 1814 an especially splendid ball to celebrate the defeat and exiling to the island of Elba of the Emperor Napoleon.

Etienne Levasseur, *The Londonderry Cabinet*, c.1775
(w. 602cm) [P390]

The enormous Boulle marquetry bookcase stretching the length of one wall is known as the *Londonderry Cabinet*. Made around 1775, it was bought in 1817 in Paris by Lord Yarmouth (later the 3rd Marquess of Hertford) for Carlton House, the London residence of his friend the Prince of Wales (later George IV). Later sold from the Royal Collection, the 4th Marquess of Hertford acquired it in 1869 from the Londonderry Collection.

The Wallace Collection has an important library and archive full of valuable information which helps us understand better the history of the collection and the family. Among the books housed in the *Londonderry Cabinet* are several from the library of the Marquesses of Hertford, embossed in gold on the spine with the family crest (see detail).

Attributed to André-Charles Boulle, Wardrobe, c.1700
(h. 255cm) [F61]

The imposing wardrobe is veneered with brass and turtleshell Boulle marquetry in a symmetrical design. Gilt-bronze† groups illustrate stories from Ovid's *Metamorphoses.*† On the left, Apollo, the sun god, pursues Daphne who is transformed into a laurel tree by her river-god father. On the right, Apollo orders the Scythian, who has a knife between his teeth, to flay Marsyas, who is bound to a tree. Apollo beat Marsyas in a musical contest, the winner of which was entitled to inflict his chosen penalty on the loser.

Philippe Bertrand, *Allegory Commemorating the Accomplishment of the Vow of Louis XIII*, 1714,
(h. 46.9cm) [S176]

The allegorical figures in this imposing group represent Religion, Piety and, blowing on a trumpet, Fame. They hold medals of Louis XIV and his father Louis XIII, who had made a vow 60 years earlier to rebuild part of Notre-Dame, Paris, if he was granted a son. The bronze group was the prize in a poetry competition, organized to commemorate the accomplishment of this vow in 1714. The winner was the now forgotten Abbé du Jarry, the indignant runner-up the young Voltaire.

The Oval Drawing Room

Boucher and Fragonard

The Oval Drawing Room is an intimate setting for the rococo paintings of Boucher and Fragonard. Two iconic French paintings, Boucher's *Madame de Pompadour* (1759) and his pupil Fragonard's *The Swing* (c.1767), face each other, inviting comparisons between the two beautiful women in pink dresses in bosky woods. The furniture represents the transition between rococo and neo-classical which can be seen in the form and decoration of Riesener's stunning roll-top desk in the centre of the room.

c.1890

Known then as the Octagon Room, this room was used by the 2nd Marchioness of Hertford as an entertaining room and ballroom. The chimneypiece, c.1785, is the only original one to survive in situ in Hertford House. Sir Richard Wallace displayed his impressive collection of miniatures here.

François Boucher, *Madame de Pompadour*, 1759
(91 x 68cm) [P418]

Madame de Pompadour stands in a garden accompanied by her spaniel, Inès. A contemporary described Madame de Pompadour, 'Her eyes have a particular charm which perhaps derives from their uncertain colour...'. The setting evokes the park at Bellevue, Madame de Pompadour's château, where 'roses, jasmine and even orange trees ... seemed to spring from the bosom of the earth.' By 1759, Madame de Pompadour's relationship with the King was platonic,

a state of affairs referred to by the statue, *Friendship Consoling Love*. Madame de Pompadour's fidelity is emphasised by her dog; as Inès is faithful to her mistress, so her mistress is faithful to the King.

Boucher (1703–70) epitomised the inimitable style of mid 18th-century French art at a time when most of Europe sought to follow the French Court and Paris. In his later years his work attracted criticism at the Salon[†], but his career did not suffer, because from 1750 he benefited from the lavish patronage of Madame de Pompadour. Boucher also created designs for tapestries, stage sets and porcelain groups. In 1755, he became the artistic director in charge of design at the Gobelins tapestry factory.

Jean-Honoré Fragonard, *The Swing*, 1767
(81 x 64.2cm) [P430]

The Swing is Fragonard's most famous painting. One critic
wrote 'the grace of its execution and the tact of the artist
excuse the sauciness of the subject'. A tantalising girl,
delicious in her froth of pink silk, is poised in mid-air beyond
the reach of both her elderly husband and her glowing lover.
The fantastical park-landscape provides an ideal setting.
A statue of *Love* makes the viewer party to the adulterous
deception by holding his finger to his lips. The flirtatiously
discarded slipper adds the perfect note of artful abandon.

The dramatist Collé related the story behind *The Swing*;
the history painter Doyen was summoned by an unnamed
'gentleman of the Court' to attend him at his pleasure
house. The gentleman pointed to his mistress and said
'I should like you to paint Madame on a swing pushed
by a bishop. Myself you will place in a position where
I can observe this charming girl's legs, and more still
if you wish to enliven your picture further'. Doyen was
rendered speechless by the libertine proposal. However, he
recovered sufficiently to suggest that the picture would be
rendered yet more agreeable by the addition of Madame's
slippers flying through the air and that Fragonard, rather
than himself, would be the best man for the job. (Fragonard
does not in the end make any reference to the Church
in his composition.) The identity of the racy patron who
adores his mistress from the undergrowth is uncertain. The
first known owner of *The Swing* was the receiver general,
Ménage de Pressigny, who was guillotined in 1794.

Jean-Henri Riesener, Roll-top desk,
c.1770 (w. 195.5cm) [F102]

The top of the desk rolls back to reveal drawers, sliding trays and a writing surface fitted with velvet-lined panels. The desk is veneered with pictorial marquetry of holly, walnut, ebony,[†] box and sycamore. On the top, letters in French and German lie amongst notebooks, one with an elaborately marbled cover; also a seal with the arms of the comte d'Orsay (the desk was supplied for the Hôtel d'Orsay in Paris), quill pens, a stick of sealing wax, a pen-knife, an inkwell, a sand box and three sponges. A personification of Silence, a young woman holding her finger to her lips, is on the back of the desk. On her left is a terrestrial globe with the attributes of geometry, including a protractor and a half-rolled map. On the right is a celestial globe with the attributes of astronomy, including a half-rolled chart and a telescope. The desk closely follows the design of Oeben's and Riesener's roll-top desk for Louis XV.

Riesener (1734–1806) was the most successful cabinet maker of the Louis XVI period and perhaps the best of all French furniture makers. Born in Germany, Riesener joined Oeben's workshop in Paris. He became the manager on Oeben's death, ousting his rival, Leleu, and four years later he married Oeben's widow. In 1774 he was appointed Cabinet maker to Louis XVI. He survived the French Revolution and was employed by the new government to remove royal emblems from furniture.

Pierre Gouthière, *The Avignon Clock,* 1771
(h. 68.5cm) [F258]

The Avignon Clock is a gilt-bronze[†] mantel clock. A personification of the city of Avignon stands to the left of the dial crowning the coronet and coat of arms of the marquis de Rochechouart. He was governor of Avignon for six years until 1774, when the city was handed back to the Pope by Louis XV. Some citizens were so delighted with the marquis' governorship that they gave him *The Avignon Clock*. Avignon is recognisable by her crown, made from the walls of the city. Beneath her, personifications of the river Rhône and the river Durance, which join west of the city, recline on a rocky hill with river water flowing from their urns. The Rhône, on the left, appears to be in conversation with the youthful Durance, who bends and uproots a sapling with the force of her current.

Jean-Baptiste Boulard, Chair, 1786 (h. 93.4cm) [F233]

The chair is one of a set made for Louis XVI's card room at the royal palace of Fontainebleau. Chairs with separate cushions were intended for ladies. It is covered with blue patterned silk, an exact reproduction of its original covering.

The Study

Louis XVI and Marie-Antoinette

*c.*1890

The Study is a feminine, comfortable, boudoir-like room celebrating Queen Marie-Antoinette of France. There are more pieces of her furniture in here than in any other room in the world. These are surrounded by portraits of people, or by artists, whom she would have known, as well as by Sèvres porcelain and other French decorative arts from the second half of the eighteenth century, when the new more austere and linear Neo-classical style supplanted the light airiness of the Rococo.

The Study was Sir Richard Wallace's private room for writing letters and reading. The photograph of *c.*1890 shows that he had the room decorated with watercolours, whilst an impressive Boulle armoire was flanked by marble busts of Sir Richard's wife and his father, the 4th Marquess of Hertford.

Pierre Gouthière, Perfume burner, 1774–5
(h. 48.3cm) [F292]

The perfume burner is an outstanding example of the work of Gouthière. A gilt-bronze serpent twists through the legs of the gilt-bronze tripod which supports a red jasper† bowl. The perfume burner was in the possession of Marie-Antoinette in 1783, the year in which her private study at Versailles was redecorated with white and gold panelling incorporating gilded carvings of perfume burners on tripods with aromatic smoke wafting from their bowls.

When the French Revolution began, Marie-Antoinette tried to safeguard her treasures, including the perfume burner, by entrusting them to various Parisian shopkeepers and dealers who had served her. Her actions were in vain as she was executed in 1793.

Gouthière (1732–c.1812) was the greatest gilder on metal of the Louis XVI period. He perfected a new process of gilding whereby parts of a gilt bronze could be given a matt finish to contrast with the burnished parts.

Elizabeth-Louise Vigée Le Brun, *Madame Perregaux*, 1789 (98.5 x 77cm) [P457]

Vigée Le Brun (1755–1842) had beauty and style which aided her professional success. She first painted Marie-Antoinette in 1778. It was partly due to the Queen that she was received by the French Royal Academy in 1783. She left Paris in 1789, escaping the French Revolution. She visited London and stayed briefly in Portman Square, next to Manchester Square where the 2nd Marquess was residing in Hertford House.

Perhaps by Antoine-François Lebrun,
Queen Marie-Antoinette and King Louis XVI, c.1775
(h. 13.3cm) [S392-3]

Jean-Honoré Fragonard, *The Souvenir, c.1776–8* (25.2 x 19cm) [P382]

In *The Souvenir* a girl carves her lover's initial, 'S', on a tree. She is observed by her spaniel, a symbol of steadfast fidelity. Notice the girl's delicately drawn profile, the calligraphic traceries of hair and foliage and the theatrical lighting. The use of panel, the scale and the careful technique show Fragonard catering for the 18th-century taste for the 'little masters' of the 17th-century Netherlands and his reference to eighteenth-century sensibility.

Ice-cream cooler, Sèvres porcelain, 1778 (h. 23.7cm) [C478]

Ice cream or sorbet would be contained in an inner liner, kept cool by packed ice in the outer bowl and in the top of the cover, as indicated by the frozen icicle handle. This is one of ten ice-cream coolers made for the Empress Catherine II of Russia and included in her remarkable dinner and dessert service of 797 pieces which was sent to St Petersburg in 1779.

Tray, Sèvres porcelain, 1778 (w. 48cm) [C407]

This tray is made of hard-paste porcelain, which was in general production at Sèvres by 1772. Part of a tea service, it shows chinoiserie scenes, here with guns blazing in a marine battle scene, with sea monsters attacking the poor sailors who have fallen into the water.

Vase and cover, Sèvres porcelain, 1768
(h. 54.4cm) [C306]

This apparently unique vase is one of the Sèvres factory's most idiosyncratic neo-classical forms. Models of vases in the new style, based on classical antiquity and the antithesis of the rococo which it superceded, were first introduced in 1763, but this example, with its tall columnar neck emerging from a Vitruvian scroll at the bottom and capped by a Greek-key pattern at the top is particularly, and with quirky zig-zag folded handles, is extraordinary.

Cup and saucer, Sèvres porcelain, c.1779
(h. 7.6cm) [C350]

The cup is painted with a portrait of Benjamin Franklin and the saucer with a trophy which includes an American Indian feathered head-dress. It celebrates the Franco-American Alliance of 1778, when Franklin succeeded in persuading Louis XVI to recognise the American Colonies and their independence from Britain.

Benjamin Franklin was sent to Paris in 1776 to persuade Louis XVI to recognise American independence from Britain. He had to wait over a year and was beloved by Court ladies and Parisian intellectuals alike. The King ratified American independence in 1777. The Sèvres factory produced busts and portrait medallions of Franklin which were copied throughout Europe.

Neo-classicism, which superseded the rococo, began to emerge in France in the 1750s. The new taste was shaped and stimulated by recent excavations at Herculaneum and Pompeii. It is characterised by the use of Greek and Roman architectural ornament, by a preference for sober colours and by linear, rather than richly sculptural, decoration.

Jean-Henri Riesener, Secretaire (writing desk), 1783
(h. 139.6cm) [F302]

The secretaire was supplied by Riesener for Marie-Antoinette at the Petit Trianon. The front drops down to form a writing surface and papers can be kept secret (hence 'secrétaire') in drawers and compartments concealed behind the doors. Richest of all the Riesener furniture in the Study, the secretaire is veneered with a stunning fret pattern enclosing holly inlaid with waterlilies of stained sycamore. The gilt-bronze plaque on the top drawer shows two naked infants sitting on clouds by a brazier. One strokes a spaniel while the other holds out a letter to Mercury, messenger of the gods, who wears a winged cap and ties winged sandals to his feet.

The Boudoir Cabinet

Gold boxes and miniatures

This intimate Cabinet houses the miniature arts of the seventeenth and eighteenth centuries, with miniature paintings, gold boxes and other luxury items.

Miniatures had a strong personal and emotional meaning. Portraits were given as a sign of love or friendship and kept by their owners as tokens of attachment or political allegiance. They could also serve as a souvenir of favourite places or important events. Many of the most important miniature painters of the period are represented in the collection. An outstanding group of works by the Swedish-born miniature painter Peter Adolf Hall shows his extraordinary genius to develop miniature painting from a meticulous description of reality into a freer, more painterly medium.

Gold boxes, usually for snuff, were deliciously extravagant personal toys which reflected the latest fashion in shape, materials and decoration. While some incorporate lacquer, turtle-shell piqué work, abalone shell, rock crystal, lapis lazuli, agate, Sèvres porcelain and vellum, others have pictorial scenes created from four-colour golds, and many are painted in enamel colours with subjects after contemporary artists. They are both small and intensely personal objects, yet they also represent a microcosm of the arts of eighteenth-century France.

Snuff box, Jean Ducrollay, Paris, 1743–4
(w. 7.6cm) [G4]

The Ducrollay box (overleaf) is shaped like a scallop shell. It is enamelled to resemble a white peacock's fan-tail which, seen from the back, rises in full display as the cover is raised.

Snuff boxes, airtight when closed, are precisely balanced so that they can be held open in the palm of the hand without tipping. Their size and weight suggest they were for display as much as wear. Snuff was taken by men and women and was subject to complex etiquette.

Peter Adolf Hall, *The Painter's Family*, 1776,
(9 x 10.1cm) [M186]

Peter Adolf Hall was one of many Swedish artists who settled in Paris in the eighteenth century. He became the most successful miniature painter of his time in France replacing the traditionally meticulous rendering of people and objects on miniatures with a looser, more painterly style. This group portrait is Hall's masterwork. It depicts Adelaïde Hall, the painter's wife, their second daughter Lucie and Adelaïde's sister Victoire, Comtesse de la Serre.

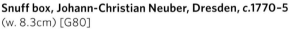

Snuff box, Johann-Christian Neuber, Dresden, c.1770–5
(w. 8.3cm) [G80]

The gold and cornelian† box by Neuber has Leda and the Swan in relief on the lid. In the base is a secret slide with, on each side, gouache† miniature portraits of Voltaire and his mistress, the marquise du Châtelet.

Snuff box, Louis Roucel, Paris, 1766–7 (w. 7.9cm) [G44]

Boxes were often enamelled with miniature reproductions of famous paintings of the day, known from Salon† exhibitions and engravings, and here the scenes are after paintings by Greuze, with his *Village Wedding* on the cover.

Gold Boxes were made and fitted together by goldsmiths but much of the decoration was undertaken by craftsmen from other guilds, such as chasers, engravers and enamellers. The whole process, from commission to delivery to the customer, might take two years.

Please be patient with the low light levels in here, but the gouache and watercolour paintings fade very fast when exposed to more light. To introduce as much light as possible, we have introduced a system which gets brighter when you approach the cases.

The Boudoir

Sense and Sensibility

The Boudoir is hung with small pictures by Greuze and Reynolds, painters who gave expression to the eighteenth-century cult of *Sensibilité* in France and England. The delicate and small-scale furniture includes a variety of writing-desks and tables appropriate for a lady's boudoir.

For Lady Wallace this was her Boudoir or private Sitting Room where she hung miniatures and small paintings on the walls, showed Sèvres Porcelain under protective glass domes on desks and tables, and displayed Sir Richard Wallace's collection of Renaissance jewellery.

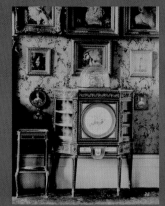

*c.*1890

Jean-Baptiste Greuze, *The Broken Mirror*, before 1763
(56 x 45.6cm) [P442]

The scene is a parable of carelessness. The disarray of the interior and the woman's dress reflect her dissolute morals. The shattered mirror symbolises the loss of her virginity. Her ringless hand and the yapping dog, a familiar symbol of carnal desire, draw our attention.

Greuze (1725–1805) was accepted by the French Royal Academy of Painting and Sculpture as a genre† painter. His moral scenes were praised by Diderot† as 'dramatic poetry to touch us, teach us, to correct us and incite us to virtue!' When the Academy rejected his history paintings, Greuze withdrew and exhibited privately in his studio. He achieved financial success with small-scale, expressive heads of young women.

Joshua Reynolds, *Miss Jane Bowles*, 1775
(91 x 70.9cm) [P36]

Jane Bowles shown as a 3- or 4-year-old girl. One account tells how Reynolds played tricks with Jane at table so that later she sat for him 'with a face full of glee.' Reynolds greatly admired Greuze, displaying a *sensibilité* akin to Greuze's portraits of small children with animals.

Adam Weisweiler, Work table, 1786–90
(h. 76.5cm) [F325]

The Empress Josephine, wife of the Emperor Napoleon I, might have kept her silk threads and fabrics on the different tiers of the work table, which belonged to her in the 1800s. The table is veneered with satinwood† laid in diamond-shapes and inlaid with dots of ebony.† The table is mounted with Wedgwood jasper-ware† cameos showing white figures against pale-blue backgrounds. The subjects are derived from classical mythology.

Jean-Jacques Caffiéri, *Cupid Vanquishing Pan*, 1777 (h. 42.5cm) [S219]

The title of this elaborate bronze group, 'Love conquers All' is engraved in both Latin and French on the base. The meticulously crafted sculpture shows bestial love, in the form of Pan, God of Nature, defeated by spiritual love, represented by Cupid. The bronze was made for the Abbé Terray, a despised Finance Minister, and an important art collector.

The West Room

The Lure of Italy

This room is hung with paintings reflecting the Italian experiences of French eighteenth-century artists and with Italian works of a type fashionable with contemporary collectors in France. Many young artists

1958

were sent from Paris to Rome as pensioners of the French Academy there and, as with Claude-Joseph Vernet, their Italian sojourn often became a stepping stone to success after their return. The Mantel Clock after Michelangelo's figures of *Night* and *Day* in Florence and the elaborate silver gilt toilet service from Augsburg, herald a transition from France to a wider Europe in the following sequence of picture galleries.

Formerly Lady Wallace's Bedroom, upholstered in blue and white, this room contained Sèvres porcelain, French furniture and paintings, including Fragonard's *The Swing*.

Mantel clock, *c*.1775 (w. 100.7cm) [F268]

The mantel clock is a neo-classical version of a model by André-Charles Boulle created in the early years of the 18th century. The bronze figures of Night and Day, which recline against the dial, are based on figures by Michelangelo. The female figure of Night sleeps with her left arm resting on a bearded mask. An owl perches in the hollow of her leg.

Silver-gilt service, Augsburg, 1757–73 (mirror h. 83cm)

In 1773, it would not have seemed incredible for a very fine lady to have need of fifty-five pieces of silver-gilt[†] in order to rise, partake of a light breakfast and write a short letter. This service, probably given as a betrothal or wedding present, would have been on show when its owner performed her morning toilette before an audience of favoured guests.

René Dubois, commode (chest of drawers), *c*.1760 (w. 157.5cm) [F245]

The Dubois commode has a single drawer in front and two side cupboards. The eccentric mix of neo-classical elements, such as sirens, and oriental elements, such as Chinese fretwork and Japanese lacquer,[†] is typical of the period. The lacquer, dyed black, has been built up in relief and gilded.

Lacquer wares were imported into Europe from China and Japan and pieces of lacquer were often incorporated into European furniture. Lacquer was extremely expensive and was reused in new pieces of furniture. In consequence, pieces which originally belonged to different panels were sometimes jumbled together in a collage. If you look at the drawer front of the Dubois commode, you will see that it is made up of small pieces which bear no relation to each other. Dubois has used the gilt-bronze fretwork to hide the joins.

Studio of Louis-Michel Van Loo, *Louis XV, c*.1759 (136.6 x 104cm) [P477]

Van Loo painted a state portrait of the King and then made a reduced-size replica to be used as a model by copyists. Numerous copies, of which this painting is an example, were given by the King to foreign royalty, and loyal friends and relations. One was owned by Madame de Pompadour.

The West Gallery I

The Wallace Collection owns an outstanding collection of
Venetian views by Antonio Canaletto and Francesco Guardi. Some
of Canaletto's paintings were acquired by the 1st Marquess of
Hertford and mark the beginning of art collecting in the family.
Canaletto and his workshop were mainly working for tourists
visiting Venice in the eighteenth century but the artists also
spend several years in England. Due to the huge demand for his
works Canaletto worked with numerous assistants and workshop
members. A close comparison of the paintings reveals notable differences in style and
quality. Antonio Guardi, born fifteen years after Canaletto, moved from exact topographical
views to more atmospheric renderings of the Laguna and became a particular favourite of
nineteenth-century collectors such as the 4th Marquess of Hertford.

1900-05

This room was created in 1897 from Sir Richard Wallace's Dressing Room, Lady Wallace's
Bath Room and Dressing Room and a corridor.

Canaletto, *Venice: the Bacino di San Marco from the Canale della Giudecca, c.1735–44* (130.2 x 190.8cm) [P499]

Canaletto, *Venice: the Bacino di San Marco from San Giorgio Maggiore,* **c.1735–44** (129.2 x 188.9 cm) [P497]

The pair of unusually large views by Canaletto look across the Bacino di San Marco from opposite directions. *The Bacino from the Canale della Giudecca* (overleaf) shows the view from the mouth of the Giudecca Canal looking across the Bacino towards the church of San Giorgio. On the left is the Dogana (Customs House) surmounted by a golden globe with a figure of Fortune. Between 1725 and 1740, Canaletto specialised almost exclusively in views of Venice. They were much sought after by English Grand Tourists who wished to take home a souvenir of the cosmopolitan city where West met East.

Francesco Guardi, *Venice: San Giorgio Maggiore with the Giudecca and the Zitelle,* **late 18th century** (68 x 90cm) [P491]

Four views of Venice by Francesco Guardi are typical of the limpid atmospheric views for which he is famous. They form two distinct pairs but were acquired by the 4th Marquess of Hertford in the 19th century as a quartet in matching frames. *San Giorgio Maggiore with the Giudecca and the Zitelle* looks across the Bacino towards the church of San Giorgio and the Benedictine monastery.

Francesco Guardi, *Venice: Santa Maria della Salute and the Dogana,* **late 18th century** (68 x 90cm) [P503]

Its companion piece, *Santa Maria della Salute and the Dogana,* shows a view from the Grand Canal towards the Dogana with the church of Santa Maria della Salute on the right. Rather than constructing idealised topographical views as Canaletto had done, Guardi here attempts to capture the magical atmosphere of Venice, where mundane details are sacrificed to a shimmering vision.

The West Gallery II

Bonington, Delaroche and Delacroix

The room, created in 2010, houses paintings by the brilliant generation of British and French painters who came to maturity during the 1820s. After thirty years of turbulence in France, culminating in the collapse of the Napoleonic Empire, many painters began to seek new inspiration from earlier European history and legend, and from literature which offered an alternative to the classicism promoted by the French academic system.

c.1890

In Sir Richard Wallace's day this space was occupied by part of his European Armoury.

Richard Parkes Bonington, *Henri IV and the Spanish Ambassador*, **1827–8** (38.4 x 52.4cm) [P351]

Richard Parkes Bonington, *Henri IV and the Spanish Ambassador,* 1827-8 (38.4 x 52.4cm) [P351]

Henri IV and the Spanish Ambassador (overleaf) depicts an anecdote from the life of Henri IV, King of France 1589–1610. He plays piggy-back with his children watched by Queen Marie de Médicis. The Spanish Ambassador, standing on the right, is clearly startled by the want of kingly behaviour. Bonington has based the faces of the King and Queen on historical portraits. His approach to history painting was more light-hearted than that of many of his French contemporaries.

Paul Delaroche, *The State Barge of Cardinal Richelieu on the Rhône,* 1829 (56.4 x 97.5cm) [P320]

This pair of paintings by Delaroche, shows the dying moments of the two cardinals who dominated French history during the first half of the 17th century.

The State Barge shows Cardinal Richelieu, Louis XIII's chief minister, travelling up the Rhône. He tows the marquis de Cinq-Mars and François-Auguste de Thou, guarded by soldiers with halberds, in a smaller boat behind. The prisoners had conspired to overthrow the Cardinal and, though mortally ill, he was determined to escort them to Lyons for their execution. He died less than three months later. The sheer extravagance of Richelieu's silk-draped barge is emphasised by the rich oriental carpet which trails in the water.

Ferdinand-Victor-Eugène Delacroix, *The Execution of the Doge Marino Faliero,* 1825-6 (145.6 x 113.8cm) [P282]

Delacroix's painting shows the execution in 1355 of Marino Faliero, Doge of Venice, punished for conspiring against the Venetian state. The subject is taken from a tragic poem by Byron, published in 1820. The decapitated body of Faliero lies at the foot of the stairs. At the top, a Venetian senator holds aloft the instrument of death, a bloody sword. The figures are dressed in 16th-century costume despite the 14th-century tale. Some are derived from paintings by Venetian Renaissance artists. *The Execution* was painted while Delacroix was sharing a Paris studio with his English friend, Bonington.

Paul Delaroche, *Cardinal Mazarin's Last Sickness,* 1830 (57.2 x 97.3cm) [P314]

The Last Sickness shows the worldly Cardinal Mazarin on his deathbed. He was chief minister during the minority of Louis XIV and rose to a position of wealth and power equalled only by his predecessor, Richelieu. Card players sit at a gaming table by Mazarin's bed and his niece plays his card for him. The Spanish Ambassador, a solemn man in black, bows to the Cardinal. The room hums with gossip and intrigue.

The Nineteenth-Century Gallery

French Nineteenth-Century Pictures

The Gallery is hung densely, as was characteristic of Sir Richard Wallace's lifetime, with paintings by nineteenth-century artists, evoking the Salons and private collections of the period. Some of these painters were acquaintances of the 4th Marquess and Richard Wallace. The 4th Marquess's interest in the Emperor Napoleon can be seen in a large collection of paintings and other works of art illustrating Napoleon and his life.

c.1890

During Sir Richard Wallace's lifetime, this room was part of the European Armoury and housed much of his collection of European arms and armour.

Ary Scheffer, *Francesca da Rimini*, 1835 (166.5 x234cm) [P316]

Ary Scheffer, *Francesca da Rimini*, 1835
(166.5 x 234cm) [P316]

The subject of *Francesca da Rimini* (overleaf) is taken from Dante's *Inferno*, a medieval epic poem. Dante makes a journey through hell with Virgil, the Roman poet, as his guide. They come upon the tragic figures of Paolo and Francesca, who are condemned to the stormy darkness of Hell's second circle with the other souls of the lustful. Francesca had been forced into marriage with the hideous Gianciotto da Rimini but fell in love with his younger brother, Paolo. Gianciotto caught the lovers while they were reading the romance *Sir Launcelot and Queen Guinevere*. He stabbed them both to death – their stab wounds are clearly visible.

Anatole Demidoff, Prince of San Donato, was a contemporary of the 4th Marquess. They were two of the most extravagant collectors of the Second Empire (the reign of Napoleon III, Emperor of the French 1852-70). The 4th Marquess was a friend and supporter of Napoleon III, whose son used to ride his pony in the grounds of the 4th Marquess's château de Bagatelle in the Bois de Boulogne outside Paris. Demidoff owned a grand villa at San Donato, on the outskirts of Florence. In the last decade of his life he began to sell parts of his collection and the 4th Marquess acquired many of his finest works of art.

The remarkable frame was made for Anatole Demidoff, who bought *Francesca da Rimini* in 1853. At the top is the inferno of Hell; in the corners are arrows and flaming torches, symbols of love. At the bottom are the towers of Rimini; in the corners are a chain ring, for eternal love, and the book which Paolo and Francesca were reading. Around the frame are parts of Dante's text.

In the 1850s Richard Wallace frequented the salon of the beautiful Madame Sabatier (it is said that she became his mistress in 1860). There he would have associated with, among others, his friend Meissonier, the poet Baudelaire and the novelist Flaubert.

Meissonier (1815-91) was inspired by 17th-century Dutch paintings. Many collectors were delighted by the 'microscopic' perfection of the artist's 'Lilliputian' gallery. Meissonier said, 'Nowadays the only thing left for a painter is to show people the past as it was.' He owned historical costumes and a collection of arms and armour.

In Meissonier's lifetime, the social and financial élites of Paris paid huge prices for his diminutive panels. They bought directly from the artist and at auction. Early collectors included the 4th Marquess, Napoleon III, and Richard Wallace.

Ernest Meissonier, *An Artist Showing his Work*, 1850
(37.5 x 29.1cm) [P325]

An Artist Showing his Work depicts an artist, in a black coat, showing his work to a gentleman. Both wear Louis XV costume. The paintings on the walls are by Meissonier himself: there is a self-portrait in the upper centre.

Ernest Meissonier, *The Roadside Inn*, 1865
(22.4 x 19.1cm) [P328]

The Roadside Inn shows horsemen in Louis XV costume stopping at an inn for refreshments. Midday sun shines through the foliage. The sharp, bright colours and dappled shadows give the painting a sparkling, effervescent quality.

Ernest Meissonier, *Polichinelle*, 1860
(55.2 x 36cm) [P337]

The figure *Polichinelle* (Punch) was painted on a door in Madame Sabatier's apartment in Paris. When she sold her collection, the panel was cut from the door and was bought by the 4th Marquess.

Horace Vernet, *The Dog of the Regiment Wounded*, 1819
(53.1 x 64.3cm) [P607]

These pictures by Vernet were immensely popular when they were painted. It was said that engravings were 'in every shop window'. *The Dog of the Regiment Wounded* depicts a bugler and a drummer tending to a wounded

Horace Vernet, *The Wounded Trumpeter*, 1819
(53.1 x 64.4cm) [P613]

dog. Behind them thick clouds of smoke show that the battle still rages. In *The Wounded Trumpeter*, a soldier lies helpless, his trumpet by his side. His horse and his dog, keep watch over him.

Jean-Baptiste Isabey,
***Napoleon I*, 1810**
(21.5 x 17cm) [M232]

Jean-Baptiste Isabey, *The Duke of Wellington*, 1818
(14.2 x 10.8cm) [M223]

Jean-Baptiste Isabey,
***The Empress Josephine*,**
1804–9 (13.5 x 9.4cm)
[M216]

Jean-Baptiste Isabey,
The Empress Marie-Louise
***and her son*, 1815**
(17 x 13cm) [M210]

Jean-Baptiste Isabey,
***Madame Dugazon*, 1813**
(12.5 x 9.5cm) [M221]

Madame Dugazon is a portrait of a famous actress. Her face, wearing a melancholy smile, is wreathed in diaphanous veils which flutter in an imaginary breeze. This fashionable look was created by Isabey.

Jean-Baptiste Isabey,
***Self-portrait*, c.1800–5**
(16.3 x 12.6cm) [M226]

Isabey (1767–1855) was the leading portrait miniaturist of the Napoleonic era. He was introduced to Napoleon by a pupil at the school where he taught drawing and became his Court Painter in 1804. Official patronage was continued by Louis XVIII, Charles X and Louis-Philippe.

The Great Gallery

c.1890

'The Greatest Picture Gallery in Europe'
Kenneth, Lord Clark (1976)

The Great Gallery is hung, as it was in Sir Richard Wallace's lifetime, with many of the superb seventeenth-century Old Master paintings from different European schools which Wallace's father, the 4th Marquess of Hertford, and other members of the family had collected. When in 1857 the 4th Marquess wrote that 'My collection is the result of my life', he would certainly have been thinking mainly of his Old Master paintings, which remain one of the proofs of his great connoisseurship.

The top-lit Great Gallery was built by Sir Richard Wallace between 1872–5, as part of his major extension of Hertford House. He consciously conceived entering this superb space, the largest and most magnificent room in Hertford House, as the culminating point of any visit to his collections.

Nicolas Poussin, *A Dance to the Music of Time*, c.1635–6
(82.5 x 104cm) [P108]

A Dance to the Music of Time represents Jupiter's gift of
Bacchus, god of wine, to the world following complaints by
the Seasons and Time about the harshness of human life.
The dancing group represents the seasons: Autumn, who
is Bacchus, is crowned with dry leaves; Winter has her hair
in a cloth; Spring has her hair braided like ears of corn and
Summer is crowned with roses. On the right, Saturn, god of
time, accompanies the dance on his lyre. On the left a two-
headed term† depicts the youthful and mature Bacchus.
Infants play with an hour-glass and with bubbles, symbols of
the shortness and fragility of life. Apollo, the sun god, drives
his chariot across the sky to make the day, another reminder
of the passing of time. The dancers can also be identified
with the perpetual cycle of the human condition: Poverty
(Autumn) leads to Labour (Winter) who leads to Riches
(Spring) who leads to Pleasure (Summer). But an excess of
pleasure leads back to poverty and the cycle starts again.
Poussin was not interested in creating naturalistic effects
but in the universal philosophical message.

**Attributed to Ferdinando Tacca, *Hercules and a
Centaur*, mid 17th century** (h. 68cm) [S118]

In classical mythology Hercules is the personification
of physical strength and bravery. The gilt-bronze† group
Hercules and a Centaur shows Hercules wrestling with
Eurytion the centaur (half man and half horse). The
centaur was to marry Deianeira but, on the wedding
day, Hercules slew the centaur and carried off the bride.

Titian, *Perseus and Andromeda*, 1553–62
(175 x 189.5cm) [P11]

In a moment of high drama, the heroic Perseus slays the sea-dragon and saves Andromeda from certain death. *Perseus* and *Andromeda* was part of a series of six mythological scenes painted for Philip II of Spain and later belonged to Van Dyck. The 3rd Marquess bought it in 1815 and, together with the Dutch cabinet pictures in the East Galleries, it gives a strong indication of his tastes.

Rembrandt van Rijn, *Titus*, c.1657
(68.5 x 57.3cm) [P29]

Titus is a portrait by a father of his teenage son. It was painted the year after Rembrandt was declared bankrupt and the 15-year-old Titus and his stepmother, Hendrickje Stoffels, were obliged to administer the production of Rembrandts's etchings and the sale of his pictures in order to comply with guild regulations. Titus is depicted in historical robes with a gold chain, recalling 16th-century Venetian portraits. Rembrandt sympathetically captures the young man's serious gaze.

Peter Paul Rubens, *The Rainbow Landscape*, c.1636
(135.6 x 235cm) [P63]

The Rainbow Landscape shows a late summer afternoon on Rubens' country estate with peasants bringing in the harvest. This is an idealised vision of a real landscape. In 1635, the 58-year-old Rubens, who lived in Antwerp, bought a country château at Elewijt, between Brussels and Antwerp. There he spent most of the end of his life with his second wife, Hélène Fourment, whom he married in 1630 when she was 16. He celebrated his purchase and his delightful marriage with a pair of landscapes, painted for his own pleasure. The pendant[†] to *The Rainbow Landscape* is *Het Steen*, a view of the château in morning sunshine (National Gallery, London).

By 1636 Rubens had largely retired from political life except that he continued to lobby the Spanish Hapsburg rulers of the southern Netherlands. He urged them to bring an end to the conflict with the rebel North which had caused crippling damage, both physical and economic, to Antwerp and the surrounding countryside. *The Rainbow Landscape* reflects Rubens' love for his native countryside; the rainbow recalls the covenant made between God and Man after the Flood and the harvest is just reward for the labours of Rubens' countrymen.

The Rainbow Landscape and *Het Steen* became separated in the 19th century and the latter was given to the National Gallery, London. When *The Rainbow Landscape* came up for sale in 1856, the National Gallery was keen to reunite

the pair. They were decisively outbid by the 4th Marquess who paid the considerable sum of 4,550 guineas. The 4th Marquess' power in the sale room was legendary.

Salvator Rosa, *Apollo and the Cumæan Sybil*, 1650s
(173.7 x 259.5cm) [P116]

Apollo and the Cumæan Sybil is one of Rosa's finest works. The eerie calm of the landscape creates a sense of foreboding in keeping with the melancholy story from Ovid's *Metamorphoses*.[†] Apollo fell in love with the Cumæan Sybil and offered her anything she desired. She asked for as many years of life as there were grains of dust in her hand. Apollo granted her wish but she still refused his advances. In retribution he denied her perpetual youth and she lived in increasing misery for over 700 years.

Anthony van Dyck, *Marie de Raet*, 1631
(213.3 x 114.5cm) [P79]

Marie de Raet and *Philippe Le Roy* are ambitious in scale and intended to impress the viewer with the exalted social position of the people portrayed. Philippe Le Roy has all the trappings of a nobleman: fine clothes, an aristocratic pose, a sword and a hunting dog. His young wife is dressed as a fashionable member of the nobility. She clutches her fan, revealing charming innocence and vulnerability; her small dog adds a note of submissive femininity. Van Dyck had just returned from Italy and was the latest fashion in Antwerp, when he painted these pictures. The portraits represent a marvellous

Anthony van Dyck, *Philippe Le Roy*, 1630
(213.3 x 114.5cm) [P94]

collusion between artist and sitters. Van Dyck captures not only likeness but aspiration. He creates an image which matches Le Roy's ambition without making him appear *arriviste*.

Le Roy is the visual embodiment of courtly ideals as set out in contemporary etiquette books. In fact he was the illegitimate grandson of a successful gunpowder manufacturer. The purpose of his life was self-advancement and his inauspicious start was soon swept under the carpet. He bought land and feudal rights which entitled him to call himself 'Lord of Ravels'. In 1631, aged 35, he married the 16-year-old Marie de Raet, a member of the land-owning classes.

Thomas Lawrence, *George IV*, 1822
(270.5 x 179cm) [P559]

Lawrence was appointed Principal Painter to George IV
on the death of Reynolds in 1792. The King gave this
portrait to his mistress, Lady Conyngham. Lawrence
considered it his 'most successful resemblance' of the
King. Becky Sharp, in Thackeray's *Vanity Fair* (1848),
describes the portrait as 'the famous one... in a frock
coat with a fur collar, and breeches and silk stockings,
simpering on a sofa from under his curly brown wig'.

Thomas Gainsborough, *Mrs Robinson 'Perdita'*, 1781
(233.7 x 153cm) [P42]

'Perdita' is a portrait of the actress, Mrs Mary Robinson.
She sits in an atmospheric landscape with her dog. The
Prince of Wales (the future George IV) had become
infatuated with Mrs Robinson in 1779 when he saw her
playing Perdita in Shakespeare's *The Winter's Tale* at the
Drury Lane Theatre. He sent her a miniature of himself
with a paper heart inside declaring eternal love. Mrs
Robinson had the miniature set in diamonds (she holds
it on her lap in the painting). But she was soon ousted
by a new mistress. Gainsborough painted Robinson's
portrait at a time when she and the Prince tried to reach a
financial settlement after their separation.

Frans Hals, *The Laughing Cavalier*, 1624
(83 x 67.3cm) [P84]

The inscription in the top right corner of *The Laughing Cavalier* tells us that the portrait was painted in 1624 and that the sitter was aged 26. Perhaps it was painted to celebrate this enigmatic young man's betrothal: symbols of love are depicted in the embroidery on his jacket. Notice Hals' astonishing display of technique: the sensitive depiction of the facial expression, which suggests that the man is party to an amusing secret; the defiant execution of the sheen of satin and the different treatments of lace – compare the delicate perfection of the cuffs with the bravura dash of the ruff.

Hals had been a successful portrait painter in Haarlem but by 1865, when this painting came up for sale, no one had heard of him. The 4th Marquess spotted the painting, called simply *Portrait of a Man*, and determined to have it. So did his friend, the baron de Rothschild, and they bid against each other. Hertford won the battle, but at a price more than six times the sale estimate. The fame of the portrait following its starring role in this sale helped reinstate Hals' reputation as a major artist and turned the painting into an icon. Its title, acquired in the aftermath of the sale, is as famous as the image despite its inaccuracy (the man is neither laughing nor a cavalier).

Bartolomé Estebán Murillo, *The Adoration of the Shepherds*, *c.*1665 (146.7 x 218.4cm) [P34]

The Adoration of the Shepherds depicts an episode in Christ's nativity. The shepherds are the first to recognise the infant Son of God. They bring doves, the traditional offering for purification after birth, and a bound lamb, symbolising Christ's sacrifice. The combination of visionary effects and realistic details, such as the shepherd's dirty foot, give the picture an immediacy typical of Murillo, whose paintings were particularly admired by the 4th Marquess.

Philippe de Champaigne, *The Annunciation*, *c.*1643–8 (334 x 214.5cm) [P134]

The dramatic austerity of *The Annunciation* reflects Philippe de Champaigne's religious sympathies (he belonged to the Jansenist faction of French Catholicism). It shows the moment in St Luke's Gospel when the Angel Gabriel announces to Mary that the Holy Spirit, symbolised by the descending dove, will cause her to bear the Son of God. Mary's abandoned work basket and *prie-dieu* (praying stool) refer to apocryphal accounts that Mary was sewing, praying or studying the prophecy of Isaiah when the angel appeared.

Diego Velázquez, *The Lady with a Fan*, *c.*1636–44
(95 x 70cm) [P88]

The Lady with a Fan is a portrait of an unknown woman, whose silent and direct gaze gives the painting a mysterious intensity. Her fan is probably *piqué*† work of gold and turtleshell. Notice the watch in the form of a crucifix hanging from her left wrist. It has traditionally been thought that she was Spanish, perhaps a member of the artist's own family. However, it has recently been argued that her dress reflects contemporary French rather than Spanish fashion and that she might be the duchesse de Chevreuse, a free-spirited Frenchwoman who sought safety from Cardinal Richelieu's regime in Spain and was painted by Velázquez in 1638.

Workshop of Giambologna, *Equestrian statuette of Henri IV*, *c.*1610 (h. 64.7cm) [S158]

The bronze *Equestrian statuette of Henri IV* shows the first of the Bourbon monarchs dressed as a military commander, mounted on a magnificent horse. It is a small version of Giambologna's over-life size bronze monument placed on the Pont Neuf in Paris in 1614 and destroyed by the revolutionary mob in 1792.

Joshua Reynolds, *Nelly O'Brien*, *c.*1762–4
(126.3 x 110cm) [P38]

Nelly O'Brien was a well-known beauty and courtesan. She was a friend of Reynolds, who used her as a model for his 'fancy pictures'. When this portrait was painted, Nelly was enjoying the protection of the 3rd Viscount Bolingbroke.

The Ritblat Conservation Gallery

The Conservation Gallery was created in the year 2000 as part of the Collection's major Millenium Project. Its permanent displays explore some of the materials and techniques involved in the construction and decoration of furniture and armour (the two principal areas dealt with by the in-house Conservation Department), and a large central exhibition space features short-term special displays highlighting various aspects of conservation, including conservation or analysis-related work carried out by the in-house conservation team as well as projects undertaken with or by the Wallace Collection's regional partner museums.

One of the most popular aspects of the Conservation Gallery, however, is the area set aside for 'armour handling'. Replica armour, together with one or two original items, are available for visitors to handle and study, or, if they wish, even wear! Some of the replica armour has deliberately been made child-sized specifically for our younger visitors to enjoy.

The Conservation Gallery's main central exhibition changes every six months. Since the gallery leads out into the Porphyry Court, where additional small changing displays can often be seen, and where the main entrance to the Exhibition Gallery is also to be found, it is always worth visiting the lower ground floor to discover what's new (and try on a Tudor breastplate while you're there!).

The Porphyry Court

The Porphyry Court was little more than a rather dismal back yard until 2000 when it was transformed by being doubled in size and provided with a dramatic pair of flights of stairs. The impressive array of porphyry vases and columns and marble busts around the walls give the area its name. The cases contain highlights from Sir Richard Wallace's superb collection of fifteenth and sixteenth-century ceramics, which is especially rich in Italian Renaissance maiolica (tin-glazed earthenware). Light-sensitive textile wall-hangings are shown in a case in the corridor alongside the Lecture Theatre.

Porphyry vase, late 17th century
(h. 72.5cm) [F363]

Porphyry is one of the hardest of all natural materials and very difficult to carve. Artefacts made from it have always been admired for their rarity and for the wonderful flecked purple-red colour of the stone. Porphyry was mined during Roman times from quarries in Egypt, which were only re-discovered in the nineteenth century. In order therefore to satisfy demand in 17th- and 18th-century France, ancient Roman porphyry columns and other objects had to be sliced up and re-carved. This vase is one of a pair in the Collection recently identified as having been made for Louis XIV.

Follower of Bernard Palissy, oval basin, late 16th century, detail (w. 49.3cm) [C174]

Workshop of Flaminio Fontana, Wine-cooler, 1574 (w. 71cm) [C107]

Most of these ceramics are formed from earthenware. The majority were made in Italy or France. They are often decorated with a subject appropriate to their function. This is true of the maiolica wine-cooler that was made in Urbino for Cosimo de'Medici, Grand Duke of Tuscany: a Roman naval battle rages in its well, which would have contained water, snow or ice to keep flasks of wine cool. The innovative French potter Bernard Palissy was fascinated by the natural world. His lead-glazed basins, moulded in relief with fish, reptiles, plants and shells like richly inhabited, fantastical ponds, inspired many imitations.

Glossary

ancien régime Political structure of pre-revolutionary France.

arabesque Rhythmic surface decoration based on patterns of scrolling and interlacing foliage and tendrils; Islamic in origin and adopted by Europeans during the Renaissance.

Arcadian Arcadia is the pastoral paradise of ancient Greek mythology.

blunderbuss Long-gun with widely flared muzzle intended to spread the shot (modern tests prove it does not).

chasing Finishing the surface of the cast metal by removing blemishes and refining detail with chasing tool.

chinoiserie Western evocations of Chinese art.

cornelian Semi-transparent quartz of deep dull red, pink or reddish white colour.

dendrochronology Method of dating wooden panels.

Diderot (1713–84) French man of letters; edited by *L' Encyclopédie* 1751.

earthenware Made of secondary clays; impurities necessitate firing at low temperature so that after firing the clay is porous.

ebony Very fine-grained jet black tropical hardwood, sometimes streaked with yellow or brown.

falchion Short sword with a broad, single-edged blade and a double-edged point.

genre Category of painting best defined in the negative; not history, religious, portrait, landscape or still-life painting, i.e. scenes with figures and without a narrative from classical mythology or history.

gilt-brass or bronze Brass or bronze with a fine layer of gold applied to the surface – see Back State Room and Conservation Gallery.

gouache Opaque water-based paint made from gum arabic and a chalk-like filler.

grotesque Fanciful decoration – 'composition for delight's sake of men, beasts, birds, fishes, flowers...'; derives from Renaissance discoveries of ancient Roman decorations in subterranean ruins known as 'grotte', hence 'grotesque'.

Japanese and Chinese lacquer Sap of the *rhus vernicifera* tree which becomes plastic on exposure to air – See Small Drawing Room.

jasper Variety of quartz, usually red, yellow or brown.

kris Characteristically-styled dagger of the Malay Archipelago.

lacquer Various kinds of resinous varnish.

mercury gilding Method of gilding metal – see Conservation Gallery.

Ovid's *Metamorphoses* Ancient Roman poem telling tales of love and the magical transformation of forms.

pendant paintings A pair of paintings.

piqué Tortoiseshell or ivory inlaid with small studs and strips of gold or silver.

Psyche In Ovid's *Metamorphoses*, Cupid falls in love with a beautiful maiden Psyche and has her brought to his palace where he visits her only after dark, forbidding her to set eyes on him.

rapier Sword with a long narrow blade and a point, for thrusting rather than cutting.

Salon The French Royal Academy of Painting and Sculpture held annual or biennial salons at which academy members' work was exhibited.

satinwood Light-coloured hardwood with a rich silky lustre, from the *chloroxylon swietenia* tree found in India and Ceylon.

shamshir Indo-Persian sword with a curved blade used for slashing cuts (also called 'scimitar').

silver-gilt Silver with a fine layer of gold applied to the surface.

term Pedestal, tapering towards the base, with bust of a human, animal or mythical figure.

triptych Picture consisting of three parts, usually a focal central element flanked by two wings.

tulipwood Tropical hardwood from the *dalbergia* tree; light coloured with a pronounced red grain resembling striped tulips.

tulwar Form of shamshir or scimitar with a characteristic style of hilt, usually Indian.

vanitas Moral warning that the acquisition of earthly treasures is mere vanity because the only certainty is death and eternal after-life, in either heaven or hell. Easily recognisable symbols ensure the message is not overlooked: candles are snuffed out like human life, hour glasses and watches remind us of the passing time, skulls need no explanation.

vellum Fine calf-skin parchment.

vernis 18th-century French imitation of oriental lacquer on wood; applied in numerous coats; lustrous with a very fine texture and a wide range of colours; perfected by the Martin brothers.

Wedgwood jasper-ware Fine-grained, slightly translucent stoneware perfected by the English potter, Josiah Wedgwood (1730–95); may be pure white or stained to a colour, e.g. the famous Wedgwood blue.